Quick & Easy
Dinners

By the Editors of Sunset Books
and Sunset Magazine

WORLD SAVINGS
AND LOAN ASSOCIATION

Lane Publishing Co. · Menlo Park, California

Foreword

Today's active people need—and demand—new ideas to reduce the time necessary for meal preparation. Within these 80 pages are menus suggesting quickly prepared, easily assembled dinners.

Each of the five chapters in this book meets different dining needs. The first chapter presents family dinners that can double as company meals. The second prepares you to entertain comfortably at small parties. Cooks who thrive on advance preparation can benefit from the make-ahead chapter. Another section offers scaled-down dinners for two. Barbecuing—a popular cooking method for both family meals and entertaining—rates a chapter by itself.

A busy cook will find many invaluable hints on timing and coordinating the meals given in the individual chapters. All the menus in this book can be prepared in 45 minutes or less—many in 30 minutes. Directions, giving step-by-step methods, explain how to prepare the dishes so that everything will be ready at the right time.

Although you don't have to serve or prepare every dish listed for any given meal, all these menus have been tested for taste compatibility. In many menus, recipes are given for the main dish and other dishes are merely suggested. You can use your own recipes or borrow suggestions from other menus to round out the meal. Use these menus as the nucleus on which to build your own balanced, quick and easy meals.

Edited by Judith A. Gaulke

Special Consultant: Kandace Esplund
Staff Home Economist, Sunset Magazine

Design: JoAnn Masaoka
Illustrations: Wendy Wheeler

Cover: Chile and Cheese Soufflé (see page 8).
Photograph by Darrow M. Watt. Design by Roger Flanagan.

Executive Editor, Sunset Books: David E. Clark

Fifth Printing March 1975

Contents

Family & Company Meals

Speedy Tortilla Pizza

Avocado-Beef Tortilla Pizza
Sour Cream
Mixed Green Salad
Fruit Bowl

A super-easy way to make pizza uses Mexican flour tortillas. All you do is brush both sides of the tortilla with olive oil, pile on the toppings, and bake in a hot oven. The crusts are thin and chewy-crisp. And you've saved all that time it usually takes to make pizza dough. Serve with green salad and fresh fruit.

Avocado-Beef Tortilla Pizza

1 pound lean ground beef
½ teaspoon salt
1 clove garlic, minced or mashed
¼ pound fresh mushrooms, sliced
1 can (about 7 oz.) green chile sauce
4 large flour tortillas (about 8-inch size)
  Olive oil
½ cup each chopped onion and green pepper
1 can (2¼ oz.) sliced ripe olives, drained
½ pound jack or mozzarella cheese, shredded
½ cup grated Parmesan cheese
1 medium-sized avocado
1 cup sour cream

Crumble the beef into a 10-inch frying pan and stir over medium heat until lightly browned and crumbly (about 5 minutes); drain any excess fat. Add salt, garlic, mushrooms, and chile sauce. Cook, stirring, over high heat until liquid has evaporated (about 3 to 5 minutes); remove from heat.

Brush tortillas lightly with olive oil on both sides—be sure edges are oiled; place slightly apart on shallow baking pans. Spread the meat sauce evenly over tortillas; then scatter the onion, green pepper, and sliced olives evenly over the tops. Sprinkle jack or mozzarella cheese in an even layer over tops of pizzas; sprinkle with Parmesan.

Bake in a 475° oven until the cheese melts and lightly browns (about 7 to 10 minutes). Peel a medium-sized avocado and cut in thin slices; arrange over tops of pizzas and serve. Pass sour cream to spoon on pizzas. Makes 4 servings.

Fresh Broiled Salmon Supper

Broiled Salmon with Mustard Sauce

Buttered New Potatoes

Fresh Green Vegetable

Wine-Glazed Fruit

The flavor of fresh salmon is so superb that even the simplest preparations suffice. Try broiling thick salmon steaks; then just before they're done, liberally spread them with a creamy, mustard-flavored sauce.

Broiled Salmon with Mustard Sauce

1 cup sour cream
½ cup finely chopped green onion
1½ tablespoons Dijon mustard
1 tablespoon chopped parsley
½ teaspoon each salt, thyme leaves, and marjoram leaves
Dash pepper
4 salmon steaks, each cut 1 inch thick
Salt and pepper

Stir together the sour cream, green onion, mustard, parsley, salt, thyme, marjoram, and pepper; set aside.

Sprinkle salmon steaks lightly with salt and pepper. To broil, line a shallow pan with foil, arrange steaks on the foil, and broil about 6 inches below a preheated broiler for 7 minutes. Remove pan from oven, turn steaks over, and spread the top of each steak generously with the cream sauce. Return to broiler and broil about 5 minutes longer or until fish flakes with a fork. Makes 4 servings.

Wine-Glazed Fruit

1 can (1 lb.) cling peach halves, drained
1 can (about 8 oz.) sliced pineapple, drained
2 bananas, cut into quarters
3 tablespoons firmly packed brown sugar
3 tablespoons soft butter or margarine
Dash ground cloves
Dash salt
¼ cup Muscatel or Port

Place fruits in a foil-lined shallow baking pan. Blend brown sugar and soft butter with cloves and salt; dot over fruits. Pour wine over fruits and broil, basting frequently, until lightly browned (about 8 minutes). Makes 4 servings.

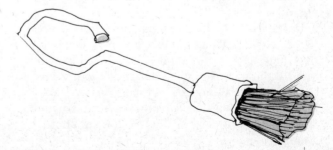

Fireside Supper

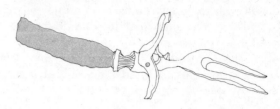

Mixed Green Salad

Steak Sandwiches with Barbecue Sauce

Baked Beans

Hot Apple Juice

Butter Oat Crisps

A blazing fire is an appropriate setting for this meal. Or serve it buffet-style from an electric warming tray.

The steak must be thinly sliced; if you ask your meatman, he can cut it for you. Keep the beans and sauce warm while you make the salad and toast the rolls; then at the last minute quickly cook the meat.

Steak Sandwiches with Barbecue Sauce

    2 pounds top round
       steak, cut across the grain in
       ¼-inch-thick slices
    About 6 rectangular
       French rolls (split, toasted,
       and buttered)
    Instant meat tenderizer
       (optional)
    About 3 tablespoons
       each salad oil and butter or
       margarine
    Barbecue Sauce (recipe
       follows)

Cut steak into pieces slightly larger than the rolls. If desired, use meat tenderizer according to package directions.

In a 10 to 12-inch frying pan, heat 1 tablespoon of the salad oil and 1 tablespoon of the butter over high heat until the fat flows in ripples when you tilt the pan. Add meat to pan without crowding, about 2 or 3 pieces at a time, and cook about 1 minute on each side or until lightly browned. Add oil and butter as needed to prevent sticking. Transfer meat as it is cooked to a platter and keep warm. As the meat stands, some juices will accumulate on the platter; add them to the sauce before serving. To serve, dip the cut side of a half roll in the sauce and top with 2 or 3 pieces of steak. Repeat to make each sandwich. Serve with remaining toasted rolls. Eat with a knife and fork. Makes 6 sandwiches.

Barbecue Sauce. Melt 1 tablespoon butter or margarine in a pan. Add ½ cup finely chopped green onion and cook until limp. Add 1 can (15 oz.) tomato sauce, 2 tablespoons firmly packed brown sugar, 1 tablespoon Worcestershire, 1 teaspoon prepared mustard, and ½ cup water; stir to blend. Heat to boiling and serve.

Butter Oat Crisps

    1 cup (½ lb.) butter
    ½ cup sugar
    1 cup all-purpose flour,
       unsifted
    1½ cups rolled oats
       (regular or quick cooking)
    1 teaspoon almond
       extract or vanilla
       Butter
       Granulated sugar
       Powdered sugar

Beat together the 1 cup butter and ½ cup sugar until light and fluffy. Stir in the flour, oats, and almond extract until well blended. Drop by rounded teaspoonfuls on greased cooky sheets about 2 inches apart.

Rub the bottom of a glass (one that has a wide, flat base) with butter. For each cooky, dip the glass into granulated sugar, then press into dough, flattening it to about ¼ inch thick. If dough sticks to glass, coat with more butter. Bake in a 375° oven until edges are light brown (about 8 to 10 minutes). Cool slightly on pans, then transfer to racks and dust with powdered sugar. Makes 4 dozen cookies.

Quick Sausage Sauté

Curried Sausage Sauté
Applesauce
Sliced French Bread
Toasted Almond Ice Cream

When you start a meal with fully cooked sausages, you have already saved one step. And these neatly encased links of spicy meat contribute the main flavoring to the dish, saving you a seasoning step. Choose fully cooked sausages, such as Polish sausage (*kielbasa*), knackwurst (garlic frankfurters), smoked sausage links, bratwurst, frankfurters, and cooked pork sausage links.

The sausage slices are sautéed in curry butter with onion and green pepper squares. Then tomatoes are added. Serve with applesauce and French bread.

Curried Sausage Sauté

About 1½ pounds fully cooked
   sausages (suggestions above)
¼ cup (⅛ lb.) butter or margarine
4 teaspoons curry powder
1 medium-sized mild white onion, cut
   in 1-inch squares
1 green pepper, seeded and cut in
   1-inch squares
2 medium-sized tomatoes, cut in
   wedges
1 can (1 lb.) applesauce

Cut sausage links on the diagonal in ½-inch-thick slices; set aside. Melt the butter in a large frying pan over medium heat; stir in the curry powder and mix well. Then add the onion and green pepper and cook, stirring, until vegetables are tender-crisp (about 2 minutes). Add the sausages and continue to cook until meat is heated through and lightly browned (about 4 minutes longer). Add the tomato wedges and stir gently for 1 minute. Turn into a serving dish and accompany with applesauce. Makes 4 to 6 servings.

Shrimp Curry in a Hurry

Shrimp Curry
Rice
Condiments
Tea
Mint Ice Cream

There's nothing to whipping together this curry dinner featuring canned shrimp on rice topped with a selection of delightful condiments. You'll need about 4 to 5 cups hot cooked rice. Serve with tasty condiments given in the recipe.

Shrimp Curry on Rice

8 slices bacon
2 or 3 hard-cooked eggs
2 tablespoons salad oil
1 medium-sized onion,
   chopped
2 teaspoons curry
   powder
1 can (10½ oz.) condensed
   golden mushroom
   soup
¾ soup can water
2 cans (4½ oz. each)
   deveined medium shrimp,
   rinsed and drained
   Rice
   Condiments (suggestions
   follow)

(Continued on next page)

Fry and crumble the bacon; then set aside. Chop the eggs and set aside.

Heat the salad oil over medium heat; add the onion and curry powder; sauté 3 to 5 minutes. Stir in the mushroom soup, water, and shrimp.

Heat through and serve over the rice. Serve the crumbled bacon, chopped egg, peanuts, toasted coconut, mandarin orange segments, and chutney in separate bowls to pass at the table. Makes 4 servings.

Cheese Soufflé Dinner

Chile and Cheese Soufflé

Buttered Fresh Asparagus

Hot Tortilla Chips

Rhubarb-Almond Pudding

This spicy soufflé, shown on the cover, will hold its volume for about 10 minutes. The extra egg yolks give it more stability.

You layer the rhubarb dessert with buttery toasted crumbs and nuts in an attractive glass serving bowl or in parfait glasses; then chill.

Warm the tortilla chips, wrapped in foil, in the oven with the soufflé the last 15 minutes of its cooking time. While the soufflé bakes, cook and season the asparagus.

Chile and Cheese Soufflé

    2 tablespoons butter or margarine
    2 tablespoons cornstarch
    1 cup milk
      Dash cayenne
    ½ teaspoon salt
    ¼ teaspoon dry mustard
      3 to 5 tablespoons finely chopped
        California green chiles (seeds and
        pith removed)
    ¼ pound sharp Cheddar cheese,
        shredded (about 1 cup)
    6 eggs, separated
    2 egg yolks

In a large saucepan, melt butter over medium heat and stir in cornstarch. Cook until bubbly. Remove from heat and gradually blend in milk, cayenne, salt, and mustard; cook, stirring, until thickened. Stir in chiles to suit your taste; add cheese and stir until melted.

Remove from heat and beat in the 8 egg yolks. Then whip egg whites until they hold short distinct peaks. Fold about half of the whites thoroughly into the sauce; then fold in remaining whites until the mixture is almost smooth. Pour into a well-buttered 1½ to 2-quart soufflè dish or casserole with straight sides. With tip of knife or spoon, draw a circle on surface an inch or so in from rim.

Bake in a 350° oven for 30 minutes or until a skewer inserted through a surface crack into the center comes out almost dry. Serve immediately or turn off oven and leave in with door closed for up to 10 minutes. Serves 4 to 6.

Rhubarb-Almond Pudding

    1¼ cups sugar
    4 cups diced fresh rhubarb
      About 4 slices firm white bread
    ¼ cup butter or margarine
    ½ cup finely chopped almonds
    1 teaspoon grated orange peel or
        lemon peel
    ⅛ teaspoon almond extract
      Whipped cream (optional)

In a saucepan, combine 1 cup of the sugar and the rhubarb; set aside. Remove crusts from bread and cut bread into ¼-inch cubes (you should have 2 cups). In a frying pan, melt butter and stir in bread cubes, almonds, and remaining ¼ cup sugar; cook, stirring, until lightly toasted. Remove from heat and stir in citrus peel. Cook rhubarb, uncovered, over medium heat, stirring until the rhubarb cooks into a sauce. Remove from heat and stir in almond extract.

In a 1-quart bowl (preferably glass) or 4 to 6 individual glasses, make a layer of half the rhubarb and cover with layer of half the crumbs; then repeat with remaining rhubarb and crumbs. Cover and chill. Top with whipped cream if you wish. Makes 4 to 6 servings.

Enchilada Dinner

Ricotta Chile Enchiladas
Slaw with Oranges and Raisins
Baked Custard

Although likened to cottage cheese, ricotta has a texture and delicate flavor all its own. You'll often find it in such Italian dishes as lasagne. Here we suggest it as a filling for enchiladas.

Ricotta Chile Enchiladas

2 cups each ricotta and shredded
    Cheddar cheese
3 to 4 tablespoons chopped canned
    California green chiles (seeds and
    pith removed)
1 tablespoon chopped pimiento
⅓ cup chopped onion
½ teaspoon salt
1 can (10 oz.) enchilada sauce
6 corn tortillas
    Sour cream

In a bowl combine the ricotta, 1 cup of Cheddar cheese, green chiles, pimiento, onion, and salt.

In a metal pie pan or small frying pan, heat the enchilada sauce until hot. With tongs, dip a tortilla into the hot sauce to cover both sides, drain briefly; then place in a baking dish (about 7 by 11 inches). Spoon about 5 tablespoons of the filling down the center of the tortilla and roll to enclose (arrange with seam side down). Repeat to fill each enchilada; top with remaining sauce.

Bake, covered, in a 375° oven for 25 minutes. Remove cover and sprinkle the remaining 1 cup shredded Cheddar evenly over the enchiladas.

Bake, uncovered, until cheese melts (about 5 minutes). Serve with sour cream to spoon over each serving. Makes 3 or 4 servings.

Slaw with Oranges and Raisins

1 quart finely shredded cabbage
¼ cup seedless raisins
2 oranges, peeled, seeded, cut in small
    pieces, or use 1 can (11 oz.)
    mandarin oranges, drained
2 tablespoons finely minced onion
⅓ cup mayonnaise
⅓ cup sour cream
    Salt to taste

Combine the cabbage with the raisins and oranges. Blend together the onion, mayonnaise, and sour cream; add to the salad and mix well, adding salt to taste. Makes about 4 servings.

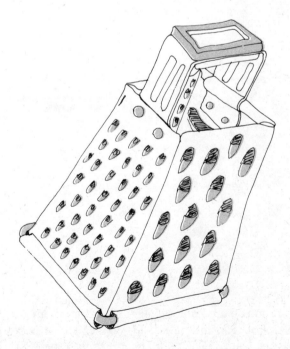

After-the-Holidays Dinner

Almond Turkey with Peas

Steamed Brown or White Rice

Butter Lettuce and Orange Salad

Oil and Vinegar Dressing

Chocolate or Rocky Road
Ice Cream

Fortune Cookies

This supper takes advantage of your leftover turkey or chicken. Another time, you might try the same entrée with cold cooked beef, pork, or baked ham instead of turkey.

Cook enough rice for 4 to 6 servings according to package directions. While the rice steams, assemble the salad. You'll need 1 to 1½ heads butter lettuce and 2 or 3 large oranges, peeled and sliced. Also have ready your own or a bottled dressing of your choice.

Since the entrée cooks at a rapid pace, have all the ingredients cut and measured before you start.

Almond Turkey with Peas

2 tablespoons butter or margarine
½ pound mushrooms, sliced
1 package (10 oz.) frozen petite peas
1 package (6 oz.) frozen edible pod peas
¾ cup regular-strength chicken broth
½ cup sliced canned water chestnuts
2 to 3 cups cold turkey or chicken cut in bite-sized pieces
⅓ cup sliced green onions
4 teaspoons cornstarch
1 tablespoon soy sauce
¼ cup roasted slivered almonds

Melt the butter over medium heat in a large frying pan or wok; add the mushrooms and sauté until golden. Add the peas, pea pods, and ½ cup of the broth; cover and cook, stirring frequently, until peas are thawed (about 3 minutes). Add the water chestnuts, turkey, and onions; cook, stirring, for 1 more minute. Combine the cornstarch, soy, and remaining ¼ cup broth; stir into turkey mixture and cook, stirring until bubbly and thickened.

Turn into a serving dish and garnish with almonds. Makes 4 to 6 servings.

Quick Egg Supper

Chard and Sausage Egg Scramble

Tomato Wedges

Hot Buttered French Bread

Few foods can match the egg as an ingredient for making quick and satisfying meals with almost universal appeal. This menu presents a new interpretation of the classic Western favorite, Joe's Special, combining mild Italian sausage and Swiss chard; serve with French bread.

Chard and Sausage Egg Scramble

½ pound mild Italian sausage
1 onion, chopped
1 clove garlic, minced
1 package (10 oz.) thawed frozen Swiss chard or chopped spinach
6 to 8 eggs, beaten
Parmesan cheese

Remove casing from sausage and crumble into a 10-inch frying pan; cook over medium-high heat until lightly browned. Add onion and garlic and cook, stirring, until onion is limp. Squeeze as much liquid as possible from chard or spinach and stir into pan; cook, stirring, until all liquid has evaporated (about 1 minute).

Pour eggs over mixture in the pan and cook, stirring, until eggs are softly set. Spoon mixture onto a serving platter. Accompany with grated Parmesan cheese to sprinkle over individual servings. Makes 6 servings.

Mexican Quesadilla Sandwich Supper

Quick Quesadillas

Tossed Green Salad

Comice Pears with Chocolate
Whipped Cream

Mexican cooks have lots of ways of stuffing a tortilla. What they call a *Quesadilla* (keh-sah-*thee*-ya) resembles our grilled cheese sandwich.

A good melting cheese is basic to all fillings for quesadillas but any other addition is at the discretion of the cook. Typically they are seasoned with chiles and onion; some also contain meat.

Our version uses flour tortillas; instead of frying, we broiled them to melt the cheese and crisp the tortillas.

Quick Quesadillas

¼ cup each shredded Cheddar and
    jack cheese
1 slice sweet onion, separated into
    rings (optional)
1 tablespoon chopped, seeded, canned
    California green chile (optional)
1 flour tortilla (about 8 inches)
    About 2 teaspoons grated Parmesan
    cheese (optional)
    About 2 teaspoons melted butter or
    margarine

Distribute Cheddar, jack, onion, and chile over half the tortilla to within ½ inch of edge; sprinkle with Parmesan. Fold tortilla over and brush top with melted butter. Turn over onto a shallow pan and brush second side with butter. Broil about 3 inches from the heat until top is lightly browned (about 2 minutes). Turn over and broil until other side is browned and cheese is melted (about 2 more minutes). Serve immediately. Makes 1.

To make spicier quesadillas, drizzle 1 tablespoon taco sauce over filling.

To substitute a different cheese, pick one that melts easily, such as Swiss, American, or teleme.

To make a meat filling, omit Cheddar or jack; add 1 slice or about ¼ cup diced cooked chicken, turkey, ham, or beef.

Comice Pears with Chocolate Whipped Cream

½ cup whipping cream
4 teaspoons ground sweet chocolate
1½ teaspoons each powdered sugar and
    orange-flavored liqueur or
    undiluted frozen orange juice
    concentrate (thawed)
2 Comice pears

In a bowl combine the whipping cream, ground sweet chocolate, powdered sugar, and orange-flavored liqueur or orange juice. Beat until stiff. Cover and chill until serving time.

Just before serving, peel, slice, and core the pears. Place in dessert bowls with tips pointing out and fill centers with cream. Makes 2 servings.

30-Minute Family Dinner

Sweet and Sour Beef
Hot Cooked Rice or Spinach
Sliced Tomatoes
Freezer Pastry or Watermelon

Versatile ground beef appears here in a well-balanced sweet and sour sauce to spoon over hot cooked rice.

If you are counting calories, omit the rice and spoon the meat mixture over hot, well-drained spinach instead. Also offer watermelon or other fresh fruit in season for dessert.

First, put the pastry (such as fruit-filled turnovers) into the oven to bake according to package directions or cut the melon into serving-sized pieces and chill until needed.

Also cook 1 cup rice or 2 packages (10 oz. each) frozen chopped spinach according to package directions. To serve, arrange rice or spinach on a rimmed platter and spoon the beef mixture evenly over top.

Since the entrée demands attention while cooking, have all ingredients handy before you start.

Sweet and Sour Beef

1 tablespoon butter or margarine
1 pound lean ground beef
1 small red bell or green pepper, seeded and cut in thin strips
1 medium-sized onion, sliced
⅓ cup firmly packed brown sugar
2 tablespoons cornstarch
¼ cup red wine vinegar
3 tablespoons soy sauce
1 can (1 lb. 4 oz.) pineapple chunks or tidbits

Melt the butter in a large frying pan over medium heat; crumble in the beef and cook until lightly browned. Add the pepper and onion and sauté, stirring often, until just tender (3 to 5 minutes).

Blend together the sugar, cornstarch, vinegar, and soy. Drain pineapple liquid into the sugar mixture and stir to blend; set pineapple aside. Stir sauce into the ground beef and cook, stirring, until thickened. Add pineapple and heat through. Makes 4 servings.

Busy Day Oven Dinner

Oven-Fried Chicken
with New Potatoes and Carrots
Lettuce Wedges
Thousand Island Dressing
Hot Fruit Turnovers   Vanilla Ice Cream

A minimum of attention is called for in preparing this meal since the chicken and vegetables bake together in the same oven. When they are done, slip frozen fruit turnovers (or homemade ones)

into the oven to bake; serve warm, topped with ice cream.

Oven-Fried Chicken with New Potatoes and Carrots

¼ cup fine dry bread crumbs
¼ cup yellow cornmeal
1½ teaspoons curry powder
¼ teaspoon salt
⅛ teaspoon pepper
    3 to 3½-pound broiler-fryer chicken, cut-up
½ cup (¼ lb.) butter or margarine
8 medium-sized carrots, peeled
8 small whole new potatoes (each about 1½ inches in diameter)
    Chopped parsley

In a small bag, combine the crumbs, cornmeal, curry powder, salt, and pepper. Shake the chicken pieces, a few at a time, in the bag and set aside. Place the butter in a large roasting pan or broiler pan (about 12 by 15 inches) in the oven while it is preheating to 400°. As soon as the butter is melted, remove pan from oven. Tilt pan slightly so butter collects in one corner; roll carrots and potatoes in butter to coat evenly and push to one side. Coat chicken with butter, laying pieces side by side with the vegetables.

Bake, uncovered, in a 400° oven for 35 minutes. Remove from oven, turn over the vegetables and chicken, return to oven, and cook for 15 minutes longer or until vegetables are tender and chicken thigh meat is no longer pink next to the bone when slashed. Arrange on a platter and garnish with parsley. Serves 4.

Broiled Ham Steak Dinner

Nut-Crusted Ham Steak
Hot Buttered Corn
Sliced Tomatoes
Berry Patch Pudding

A fully cooked ham steak that only needs heating to serve is a good choice for dinner when time is short.

Cook frozen whole kernel corn according to package directions and serve the sliced tomatoes with your favorite dressing, if desired. The dessert can be made ahead and served cold or put together just before dinner and served warm.

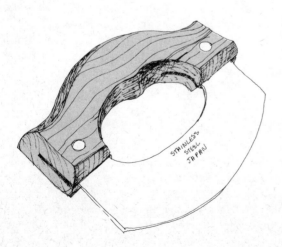

Nut-Crusted Ham Steak

Brush a ¾-inch-thick, fully cooked ham steak (about 1½ pounds) generously with honey. Broil about 5 inches below heat for 3 or 4 minutes. Turn steak, brush top side with more honey, and sprinkle with ¼ cup finely chopped salted peanuts. Broil until nut topping is lightly toasted. Carve and serve. Makes 6 servings.

Berry Patch Pudding

4 cups cleaned whole berries of your
    choice (olallieberries, boysenberries,
    blackberries, loganberries, or
    strawberries)
1 cup sugar (or to taste)
½ teaspoon ground cinnamon
¼ teaspoon ground nutmeg
2 tablespoons butter or margarine
1 cup all-purpose flour
1 tablespoon sugar
1 teaspoon baking powder
½ teaspoon salt
1 egg
½ cup milk
2 tablespoons salad oil

Butter a 2-quart shallow baking dish and fill with berries. Sprinkle with the 1 cup sugar, the cinnamon, and nutmeg. Dot with butter. Stir together the flour, the 1 tablespoon sugar, baking powder, and salt. Add egg, milk, and salad oil; beat until smooth. Pour evenly over berries. Bake in a 350° oven for 35 minutes. Serve warm or cold. Makes 6 to 8 servings.

Easy Fish Soup Supper

Mixed Green Salad

Quick Tomato Seafood Soup

Hot Crusty Bread   Butter

Toasted Pound Cake Fingers with Ice
Cream

Tomato soup is the base of this quickly prepared fish soup. It combines fresh or frozen fish with either canned or fresh crab and shrimp.

Thaw frozen fish just long enough so you can cut it into chunks. It can be added to the soup partially frozen.

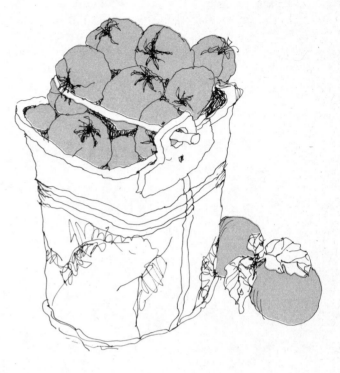

Quick Tomato Seafood Soup

    2 tablespoons olive oil or salad oil
    1 medium-sized onion, thinly sliced
    2 cloves garlic, minced or mashed
    1 cup sliced celery
    2 tablespoons chopped parsley
    1 teaspoon basil leaves
    ½ teaspoon each rosemary and thyme
       leaves
       Dash cayenne
    1 large can (26 oz.) condensed tomato
       soup
    1 bottle (8 oz.) clam juice
    1 can (about 14 oz.) regular-strength
       chicken broth
    2 ounces spaghetti
    1 pound halibut or Greenland turbot
       fillets (partially thaw if frozen), cut
       in about 1-inch chunks
    1 can (4½ oz.) small whole shrimp
       (rinsed and drained well); or use
       fresh shrimp
    1 can (8 oz.) crab meat (drained); or
       use fresh crab
       Salt and pepper
       Lemon wedges

Heat the oil in a Dutch oven over medium heat. Add onion, garlic, and celery; cook, stirring, until onion is limp. Stir in parsley, basil, rosemary, thyme, cayenne, tomato soup, clam juice, and chicken broth. Bring to boiling; break spaghetti roughly into thirds and stir into soup. Cover the pan and simmer until spaghetti is almost tender, about 10 minutes.

Add halibut; cover and simmer until halibut flakes when prodded with a fork (about 7 minutes for fresh or completely thawed fish or about 12 minutes if it was partially frozen). Stir in shrimp and crab; heat until hot throughout. Season to taste with salt and pepper.

Ladle soup from a tureen or serve in individual bowls. Offer lemon wedges to squeeze over. Makes 4 to 6 servings.

Toasted Pound Cake Fingers

Purchase 1 frozen pound cake. Cut 5 slices, each ¾-inch thick; then cut each slice in 4 lengthwise strips. Toast the pound cake pieces, turning to lightly brown all sides. Serve hot or cooled with scoops of your favorite ice cream flavor. Makes 6 servings.

Thrifty Oven Stew

Prune-Glazed Oven Pork Stew
Hot Cooked Rice
Butter-Steamed Carrots
Strawberries with Sour Cream Sauce

Compared to other meats, pork butt is usually a good buy for family meals. It's widely available (sometimes under the name Boston butt), less expensive than other cuts of fresh pork, and especially flavorful. And it doesn't require long cooking to become juicy and tender.

Use the oven to quickly brown the meat; then add a rich sauce before baking. Select a lean butt with little surface fat and ask your meatman to bone it for you.

Prune-Glazed Oven Pork Stew

About 3½ pounds lean pork butt, boned
2 tablespoons salad oil
About 12 small boiling onions
About 10 pitted prunes
1 cup prune juice
1 tablespoon lemon juice
1 teaspoon salt
½ teaspoon crushed rosemary leaves
¼ teaspoon each ground cinnamon, ginger, and pepper
1 teaspoon cornstarch mixed with 1 tablespoon water

Trim and discard excess fat; cut meat into 1-inch cubes. Place oil in a shallow baking dish (about 9 by 13 inches); set dish in oven while it preheats to 500°. Add meat and onions to pan and cook, uncovered, until meat is browned, (about 15 minutes); stir often. Add prunes to pan. Combine prune juice, lemon juice, salt, rosemary, cinnamon, ginger, and pepper. Reduce heat to 350°. Pour sauce over meat, cover, and bake 30 minutes or until meat is tender when pierced.

With a slotted spoon, transfer meat, prunes, and onions to a serving dish; keep warm. Pour the juices into a pan; skim fat. Over high heat, boil juices until slightly reduced. Add cornstarch and water and cook, stirring, until thickened. Pour sauce over meat; serve with rice. Serves 6.

Butter-Steamed Carrots

Melt 2 tablespoons butter in a wide electric frying pan set at high heat (or use a wide frying pan over direct high heat). Add 3 cups thinly sliced, peeled carrots (10 to 12 slender carrots) and 3 tablespoons water. Cover and cook, stirring occasionally, for 5 minutes. Season with salt and pepper to taste. Makes 4 servings.

Strawberries with Sour Cream Sauce

Mix until smooth 1 carton (8 oz.) sour cream and ½ cup sifted powdered sugar; stir in 2 tablespoons lemon juice and 3 tablespoons orange-flavored liqueur. Cover and chill. Pour about 2 tablespoons of the sauce over each serving of whole or sliced berries. Makes 6 to 8 servings.

Midweek Family Dinner

Sesame Liver Sauté

Buttered Green Beans

Lettuce, Bacon, and Green Onion Salad

Blue Cheese Dressing

Hot Biscuits   Butter

Butterscotch Cake with Peaches

When you are in a hurry, buy a good, bottled dressing, ready-to-bake biscuits, and frozen green beans. All are short-cuts for meal preparation.

For the salad, allow about 1 cup bite-sized pieces of iceberg lettuce, 1 or 2 slices bacon (crisply fried and crumbled) or 1 tablespoon bacon-flavored vegetable protein chips, and 1 thinly sliced green onion for each serving. Toss with dressing just before serving.

For dessert, here's a cake with a broiled butterscotch topping that goes well with fresh peaches.

Sesame Liver Sauté

    3 tablespoons butter or margarine
    2 large onions, thinly sliced
    1 pound baby beef liver, cut in
         ¼-inch-thick slices
    3 tablespoons lemon juice
    2 tablespoons salad oil
    ½ cup sesame seed
       Chopped parsley

Melt the butter in a large frying pan over medium-low heat; add the onions and cook slowly, stirring occasionally, until limp and golden (about 20 minutes).

Meanwhile, cut across each slice of liver in ½ to 1-inch strips; pour lemon juice over liver pieces and let stand for 10 minutes.

When onions are cooked, lift from pan and keep warm. Add the oil to the pan and place over medium-high heat; drain liver strips, dredge each in sesame seed (shake off excess), and sauté in the oil until liver is browned on all sides and is still slightly pink when slashed (3 to 5 minutes). Turn into a serving dish, top with the onions, sprinkle with parsley, and serve at once. Makes 4 servings.

Butterscotch Cake with Peaches

    2 eggs
    1 cup each sugar and all-purpose
         flour, unsifted
    1 teaspoon baking powder
    ¼ teaspoon salt
    ½ cup milk
    1 tablespoon butter
    ½ teaspoon vanilla
       Butterscotch Topping (recipe follows)
       Sweetened Sliced Peaches

In the bowl of an electric mixer, beat eggs until light. Add sugar, 1 to 2 tablespoons at a time, beating well after each addition. Combine flour, baking powder, and salt; sift into egg mixture and fold carefully until blended. Heat milk with butter until melted. Add to flour mixture with vanilla; fold until well blended. Turn into a greased and floured 8-inch square baking pan. Bake in a 350° oven for 35 minutes or until the top springs back when lightly touched. Remove from oven, spread with topping, and broil about 4 inches from heat until bubbly, watching carefully. Cool. Cut into squares and serve with sliced peaches. Makes 6 servings.

Butterscotch Topping. Blend 2 tablespoons soft butter with 4 tablespoons firmly packed brown sugar, 3 tablespoons milk, and ½ cup chopped pecans or filberts.

Quick Corned Beef

Corned Beef Bake
Tangy Green Beans
Garlic Buttered Rye Toast
Applesauce Crisp
Coffee or Tea

This meal centers around a creamy casserole that goes together quickly. If you are unable to find the twist-shaped macaroni, substitute elbow macaroni. Mix garlic powder with butter and spread it over buffet rye slices on a baking sheet. They will toast to buttery crispness in the oven as the casserole bakes. Before you serve dinner, combine the ingredients for the Applesauce Crisp in a baking dish you can serve from at the table. It bakes in just 20 minutes—in time to serve piping-hot as a finale.

Corned Beef Bake

    6 ounces (about 3 cups) macaroni
          twists
       Boiling salted water
    1 can (10½ oz.) condensed cream of
          celery soup
    ½ cup each milk and warm water
       Dash pepper
    1 tablespoon each dill seed and
          prepared horseradish
    1 jar (2 oz.) sliced pimiento, drained
    1 can (12 oz.) corned beef, cubed
       Buttered bread crumbs

Cook macaroni in boiling salted water until tender (about 7 minutes); drain, rinse with hot water, and drain again. While macaroni is cooking, combine soup, milk, water, pepper, dill seed, and horseradish; cover and heat to boiling, stirring occasionally. Add pimiento and corned beef. Place macaroni in buttered 1½-quart casserole; top with crumbs. Bake in a 350° oven for about 20 minutes. Makes 4 servings.

Tangy Green Beans

Heat 2 cans (1 lb. each) green beans in the liquid in which they are packed. Drain well and mix in ¼ cup prepared French dressing, 2 tablespoons butter or margarine, and a dash each of Worcestershire, salt, and pepper. Makes 4 servings.

Applesauce Crisp

Pour 1 can (about 1 lb.) apple sauce or 1½ to 2 cups canned or freshly made apple sauce (sweetened) into a shallow greased baking pan and dust top lightly with ground nutmeg; sprinkle with ¼ cup raisins and ⅔ cup crushed zwieback crumbs. Dot crumbs with 3 tablespoons butter or margarine. Bake in a 375° oven for 20 minutes or until top is lightly browned. Makes 4 servings.

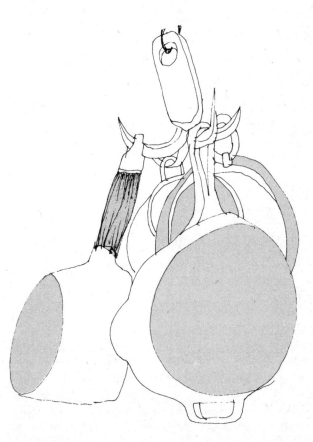

Menus for Small Parties

Tosta Party

<hr />

Tostas
Green Salad
Chilled Apple Juice and White Wine
Basket of Fresh Fruit

<hr />

This quickly managed party, ideal for impromptu festivities, has been spirited directly from the streets of Milan, where tosta grills abound. Tostas, on close inspection, are grilled ham and cheese sandwiches enhanced by savory vegetables tucked inside after the sandwiches have been toasted. You can make or buy these condiments.

In keeping with the informality of this gathering, each person cooks his own tosta. Serve a green salad, chilled apple juice and white wine; pour beverages separately or blend in the glass to make a punch. Finish the meal with a basket of fresh fruit.

Tostas

½ to ¾ pound each sliced fontina or
  tybo cheese, chunk teleme or jack
  cheese (cut off portions as needed)
½ to ¾ pound sliced cooked ham
¼ to ⅓ pound thinly sliced
  prosciutto (optional)
1 large loaf (1 lb.) sliced egg bread or
  French bread
Condiments (see below)

If you have an electric sandwich grill, group the sandwich ingredients on a low table, perhaps by the fire. If you cook the tostas in a frying pan, assemble the ingredients on a counter in the kitchen or family room.

To make a tosta, place a slice or two of cheese and meat between slices of bread. Toast in a sandwich grill on medium or high heat (or in a frying pan with a lid—even an electric frying pan—on medium heat, turning as needed) until browned and cheese melts; use no fat. Open sandwich and add any or all of the condiments. Serve tostas on plates since they tend to drip.

Tosta Condiments. Serve at least 4 of the following in separate, small dishes.

Russian dressing. Blend ⅔ cup mayonnaise with ¼ cup drained sweet pickle relish and 2 tablespoons tomato-based chile sauce; keep covered and cold until time to serve.

Red peppers. Seed and sliver 1 large red bell pepper. Cook, covered, over moderately-high heat with 2 tablespoons *each* olive oil and water until liquid evaporates. Remove cover and stir in 1 tablespoon wine vinegar and salt to taste. Serve at room temperature. (or buy 1 8-oz. jar of sweet fried peppers with onions.)

Eggplant Caponata. Open 1 can (about 5-oz. size) eggplant caponata and serve.

Pickled Peppers. Open 1 jar (about 3 oz.) Italian-style pickled peppers (peperoncini) and serve.

Onions. Peel 1 large onion and cut vertically in slivers. Place in a wide frying pan with ¼ cup water and 2 tablespoons white wine vinegar; boil and stir until liquid evaporates and onions are limp. Salt to taste and serve at room temperature. (Or buy 1 jar about 6 oz. pickled onions and slice thinly.)

Mushrooms. Thinly slice ½ pound mushrooms and sauté in 2 tablespoons olive oil until limp; add 2 tablespoons vinegar and cook until liquid evaporates. Salt to taste and serve at room temperature. (Or buy 1 jar about 5 oz. marinated mushrooms and thinly slice.)

Artichokes. Open 2 jars (6-oz. size) marinated artichokes and cut in thin slices; serve at room temperature.

Steak Sandwich Buffet

Broiled Steak Sandwiches with Beef Dip

Crusty Rolls

Vegetables with Creamy Dill Sauce

Potato Puffs

Swiss Chocolate Fondue

Easy steak sandwiches are ideal for entertaining friends after a game or other activity. Ask your meatman for the first cut off the top round (sometimes called London broil). Purchase 1 large package (about 2 lbs.) frozen potato puffs. While the steak broils, you can heat the frozen potatoes according to the package directions. Each guest fills crusty rolls with sliced beef and takes a bowl of beef dip for dunking. Accompany with vegetables in dill sauce.

Broiled Steak Sandwiches with Beef Dip

3½ to 4 pounds top round, cut 2 inches thick
2 cans (about 14 oz. each) regular-strength beef broth
2 teaspoons beef stock base or 2 beef bouillon cubes
1 teaspoon Worcestershire
About 12 crusty French rolls (split and buttered)

(Continued on next page)

Broil steak about 6 inches from the heat (about 15 minutes on each side for rare). Transfer meat to a carving board and cut across grain into thin, slanting slices; keep warm.

Meanwhile, in a saucepan combine beef broth, beef stock base, and Worcestershire; bring to boiling. Add any meat juices that have accumulated on the carving board; serve in small individual bowls. Guests fill rolls with 2 or 3 slices of meat; then dunk their sandwiches in the broth. Serves 6 to 8.

Vegetables with Creamy Dill Sauce

Combine 1 cup sour cream, ¼ cup mayonnaise, 1¼ teaspoons celery salt, 1 tablespoon dill weed, 1½ teaspoons parsley flakes, ¼ teaspoon onion powder, 1 clove garlic (minced or mashed), and ½ teaspoon prepared horseradish; cover and chill at least 2 hours. Serve with raw carrot or celery sticks, cauliflower pieces, or cherry tomatoes for dipping. Makes about 1¼ cups.

Swiss Chocolate Fondue

    12 ounces milk chocolate, semi-sweet
          baking chocolate, or other flavored
          chocolate (coffee, almond,
          hazelnut, or honey)
    ¾ cup whipping cream
    3 tablespoons Cointreau, brandy, rum,
          or crème de menthe
    2 medium-sized bananas
    1½ cups strawberries, washed and
          hulled
    1½ cups fresh (or canned) pineapple
          cubes
    6 slices angel food cake, cut about ¾
          inch thick

Place chocolate and cream in the top of a double boiler; set over hot (not boiling) water and heat, stirring, until chocolate melts and blends with cream. Stir in liqueur or liquor.

Transfer to a small pan and place over a candle warmer or electric food warmer. (Be careful not to overheat chocolate sauce, or it may scorch.)

Cut bananas into ½-inch sections and arrange on a tray with the hulled strawberries and pineapple cubes. Cut cake into bite-sized squares and add to the tray.

Place tray beside the hot chocolate sauce and accompany with bamboo skewers or fondue forks. Makes 6 to 8 servings.

Spaghetti Supper

Carbonara

Green Salad with Oil and
Vinegar Dressing

Summer Peaches with
Honey and Cream

One of the quickest and most impressive sauces for hot cooked spaghetti is the golden blend of eggs and cheese with little bits of browned meat that make Carbonara. A green salad with fruit completes the meal.

First cook the pork for the Carbonara (this can be done ahead); when it is crisp and brown, put on water for the spaghetti and make the salad.

As the Carbonara mixes together in a showy fashion, you might like to bring the ingredients to the table for the final blending.

For dessert, pass around whole peaches and let guests peel their own at the table; or if you prefer, peel the fruit ahead, but mix with lemon juice or an ascorbic acid preparation to prevent darkening.

Carbonara

    1½ to 1 ¾ pounds boneless pork butt
        (or loin end cut in ½-inch cubes,
        including fat)
    ½ teaspoon salt
    ½ teaspoon fennel seed (optional)
    4 tablespoons butter or margarine
   12 ounces spaghetti
        Boiling water
    5 eggs, well beaten
    2 cups freshly grated Parmesan cheese
    1 cup finely chopped parsley
        Pepper and salt

Mix pork with the ½ teaspoon salt and fennel seed. Cook in a wide frying pan over medium heat, stirring occasionally, until juices have evaporated and meat is well browned (about 20 minutes). To the pan, add the butter and heat until melted; keep hot. (This much can be done ahead; reheat to continue.) While the meat cooks, add the spaghetti to boiling water and cook until tender, following package directions.

Have ready the beaten eggs, Parmesan cheese, parsley, pepper and salt. (Group on a tray if you plan to assemble Carbonara at the table.)

Drain spaghetti and add at once to the hot meat sauce. Mix well (this can be done at the table). Pour in the eggs and blend, lifting and stirring the pasta. Sprinkle with half the cheese and the parsley and mix well again. Sprinkle with remaining cheese and a little pepper. Serve, seasoning to taste with salt. Makes 6 servings.

Scandinavian-Style Supper

~~~~~~

Appetizer-Salad Board
Creamed Scallops with Grapes
Patty Shells or Hot Cooked Rice
Fresh Fruit Tray   Cookies

~~~~~~

You might arrange this supper for six on three trays or platters to carry to the patio on a warm summer evening. Both the appetizer and dessert trays are assembled from items purchased at the supermarket. The third tray holds the entrée of hot creamed scallops.

On a large wooden board, arrange 1 or 2 loaves of bread and a variety of purchased appetizer and salad items. Choose from herring in sour cream or wine sauce, canned paté or liverwurst, sardines, cream cheese, pickled beets, marinated bean salad, cucumber slices, and flatbread, pumpernickel, or buffet rye.

While you are preparing the creamed scallops, bake 1 package (10 oz.) frozen patty shells as

directed on the package (or buy 6 patty shells from a bakery) or cook 1½ to 2 cups long grain rice according to package directions.

For dessert, offer a choice of fresh fruits—apricots, peaches, plums, melon wedges, berries—and mildly sweet cookies, such as Petit Beurre (butter biscuits) or Danish butter cookies.

Creamed Scallops with Grapes

        Court Bouillon (recipe follows)
    1½ pounds scallops (thaw if frozen)
    4 tablespoons butter or margarine
    1 medium-sized onion, chopped
    4 tablespoons all-purpose flour
    1 tablespoon curry powder
    1¼ cups light cream (half-and-half)
    1 teaspoon lemon juice
    4 hard-cooked eggs, diced
    1 cup seedless grapes
        Salt, pepper, and ground nutmeg
        Baked patty shells or hot cooked
        rice

Prepare the Court Bouillon. Rinse the scallops, break into bite-sized pieces, and drop into the simmering bouillon. Simmer, uncovered, for about 5 minutes or until the scallops are firm throughout. Pour the bouillon through a wire strainer, return to boiling, and boil, uncovered, until reduced to about 1 cup. Discard seasonings and set scallops aside.

In a frying pan, melt butter over medium heat; add onion and sauté until limp (about 5 minutes). Stir in the flour and curry powder and cook until bubbly. Remove from heat; gradually add the 1 cup Court Bouillon and cream; cook, stirring, until bubbly and thickened. Remove from heat

and stir in the scallops, lemon juice, eggs, and grapes; season to taste with salt, pepper, and nutmeg. Return to heat until warmed through. Serve in patty shells (pass remaining scallop mixture in a serving bowl) or over rice. Makes 6 servings.

Court Bouillon. Combine 1 bottle (8 oz.) clam juice, 1 can (about 14 oz.) regular-strength chicken broth, 1 bay leaf, 4 whole cloves, 6 whole black peppers, and ½ teaspoon thyme leaves, crumbled. Bring to a boil, reduce heat, and simmer 5 minutes.

Company Curry Dinner

Ground Beef Curry

Assorted Condiments

Spicy Okra   Steamed Rice

Sliced Cucumbers   Cherry Tomatoes

Fruit Sherbet

The authentic flavor of this curry dinner belies the simplicity of its preparation, making it an ideal choice for a small dinner party.

Ground Beef Curry

    1 large onion, finely chopped
    1 tablespoon salad oil or olive oil
    1½ pounds lean ground beef
    1 teaspoon salt
    1 tablespoon curry powder
    1 can (about 14 oz.) regular-strength
        beef broth
    2 teaspoons cornstarch
    1 tablespoon lemon juice
        About 2½ cups hot steamed rice
        Assorted condiments (suggestions
        follow)

Using a large frying pan, sauté onion in oil until golden; push to the sides of the pan. Quickly

shape meat into bite-sized balls and drop into the pan; add salt and brown on all sides. Add curry powder and sauté 1 minute. Blend 2 tablespoons of the broth with the cornstarch to make a paste; pour remaining broth into pan and bring to a boil. Stir in the cornstarch paste and cook, stirring gently, until thickened; stir in lemon juice. Turn curried meat into a hot serving bowl. Mound rice in another bowl. Serve at the table with assorted condiments (see below). Makes 4 to 6 servings.

Assorted Condiments. Place in individual bowls ¾ cup flaked coconut; ¾ cup salted cashews, chopped; 1 small cucumber, chopped; and 1 can (about 9 oz.) pineapple tidbits, drained.

Spicy Okra

Thaw 2 packages (10 oz. each) frozen okra. Cook in a small amount of boiling salted water just until tender when pierced. Rinse with cold water and drain well. In a frying pan, melt 4 tablespoons butter or margarine; add 1 medium-sized onion (chopped) and cook, stirring, over medium heat until limp. Stir in 1 teaspoon ground turmeric and cook, stirring, for 1 minute more. (Cover and set aside for up to several hours if done ahead.) Stir in the okra and 1 tablespoon white wine vinegar. Cover and cook over medium heat for 2 minutes or until hot through; shake pan occasionally. Makes 6 servings.

Holiday Chicken Dinner

Chicken in Sweet Cream
Savory Rice
Buttered Green Beans
Butter Lettuce Salad
Oil and Vinegar Dressing
Lattice-Topped Cherry Pie

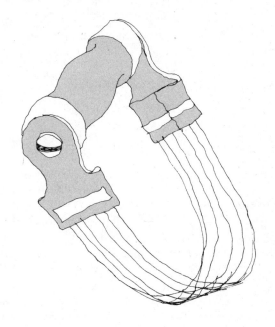

For company showmanship, you can flame the chicken just before serving.

Bake the pie early in the day to serve with vanilla ice cream, if desired.

For the rice, prepare 1 package (6 oz.) chicken-flavored rice mix according to package directions. Just before serving, garnish with avocado slices and toasted diced or slivered almonds.

Chicken in Sweet Cream

4 to 5 pounds chicken parts (breasts and thighs)
Salt and pepper
2 tablespoons butter or margarine
½ cup regular-strength chicken broth
¼ cup dry red wine or apple juice
2 tablespoons cornstarch
1 cup whipping cream
⅓ cup brandy (optional)

Rinse chicken pieces and pat dry; season with salt and pepper. In a frying pan, melt butter over medium heat; brown chicken pieces, a few at a time, on both sides. Set breasts aside. Arrange thighs in pan, add chicken broth and wine, cover, and simmer 15 minutes. Add breasts, cover, and simmer 10 to 15 minutes longer or until juices run clear (cut a gash to test). Arrange chicken in a serving dish; keep warm. Combine cornstarch and cream; add to pan juices and cook, stirring until bubbly and thickened. Pour over chicken.

For flaming, heat measured brandy quickly to bubbling, ignite, and pour slowly over chicken; spoon sauce over chicken until flames die. Serves 6 to 8.

Lattice-Topped Cherry Pie

2 cans (1 lb. each) pitted sour cherries
⅓ cup granulated sugar
⅓ cup brown sugar, firmly packed
⅛ teaspoon almond extract
2½ tablespoons cornstarch
Pastry for a two-crust 9-inch pie
1 tablespoon butter or margarine

Drain cherries, saving ⅓ cup of the liquid. Combine cherries, reserved liquid, granulated sugar, brown sugar, extract, and cornstarch. Stir well; set aside.

Prepare the pastry from your own recipe or pie crust mix. On a floured board, roll out half the pastry to fit a 9-inch pie pan. Roll out remaining pastry the same size; then cut into ½-inch-wide strips. Set strips aside.

Pour cherry mixture into pastry; dot with butter. Arrange pastry strips, about ½ inch apart, across the top in a lattice fashion. Crimp edges decoratively to secure strips. Bake in a 375° oven for 40 minutes or until crust is golden and juices are bubbly. Cool. Makes 6 to 8 servings.

Steak and Onion Dinner

Flank Steak with Onion Cream
Boiled New Potatoes
Green Vegetable
Almond Tart

A rich sauce of sour cream and onions can be used as a creamy topping for an entire, quick-to-assemble dinner. Broiled flank steak, boiled new potatoes, and a green vegetable, such as asparagus, green beans, or broccoli all share this flavorful topping and make a handsome meal presented on a carving board.

The potatoes in their skins take about 30 minutes to cook. Cover them with water and boil while you sauté the onions. A rare steak broils in 10 to 12 minutes. During this time the green vegetable can cook.

Frozen puff patty shells are the short-cut secret to the swift assembly of the multi-layered Almond Tart for dessert. The recipe makes enough for two meals.

Flank Steak with Onion Cream

6 tablespoons butter or margarine
3 large onions, thinly sliced
½ teaspoon salt
1 cup sour cream
1 flank steak (about 1½ lbs.)
8 small hot, boiled new potatoes
    (about 1½ lbs.)
  About 1½ pounds asparagus,
    broccoli, or green beans, cooked
    and hot
  About 1 tablespoon minced parsley

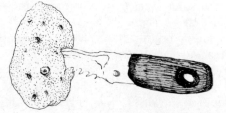

Melt the butter in a wide frying pan. Add the onions and cook, stirring, over medium to medium-high heat until onions are limp and golden; it takes 20 to 30 minutes. Stir in the salt and sour cream. Remove the pan from heat and keep warm.

Meanwhile, broil the flank steak 3 inches from the heat; allow about 5 to 6 minutes on each side for rare meat. Place meat on carving board, arranging potatoes and asparagus around it. Pour sauce into a small bowl and sprinkle with parsley.

To serve, cut thick slanting slices diagonally across the grain of the steak. Spoon onion cream over individual portions of meat and vegetables. Makes 4 servings.

Almond Tart

1 package (10 oz.) frozen puff patty
    shells, thawed
1 cup blanched whole almonds
½ cup sugar
2 eggs
3 tablespoons soft butter or margarine
¼ teaspoon almond extract
1 teaspoon grated lemon peel
3 tablespoons powdered sugar

Allow frozen patty shells to warm almost to room temperature.

For filling, whirl almonds in a blender until you have the consistency of cracked wheat. Turn into a bowl; add sugar, 1 egg, the yolk only of second egg, butter, almond extract, and lemon peel. Beat until blended and creamy.

On a lightly floured board, arrange 2 patty shells, with edges touching. Cut a third shell in half and place outside edges next to the 2 whole shells to form a rough circle; pinch edges together. Roll out into a 10-inch circle. Repeat with remaining 3 shells, making a second circle.

Place 1 circle of puff paste on an ungreased baking sheet. Spread with filling to within 1 inch of the edge. Top with remaining pastry. With a fork, seal the outer edge; then cut decorative slashes across top layer of pastry. Brush top with remaining egg white, lightly beaten. Sift powdered sugar evenly over top. Bake in a 450° oven for 20 minutes; reduce temperature to 400° and bake 10 minutes longer or until well browned. Serves 8.

Skewered Shrimp Dinner

Dramatically skewered shrimp, broiled pink and juicy, combine with hot artichokes to make a handsome main course. Both are dipped into garlic butter as you eat.

As served in Italy, France, Spain, and Mexico, these shrimp are typically cooked in their shells. Many feel that the flavor is the sweetest when prepared in this manner, but the shrimp are messy to eat, so you may prefer to shell them before cooking. Our recipe gives both alternatives.

Cook the rice for the salad a few hours before mealtime and allow it to cool to room temperature. You can also clean and skewer the shrimp early and keep them cold.

While the artichokes cook, make the Garlic Butter Sauce; then broil the shrimp. Buy a frozen orange cake or bake one for dessert; serve with fresh orange slices.

Skewered Shrimp with Garlic Butter Sauce

    2 pounds shrimp (30 to 40 to the lb.)
    ½ cup (¼ lb.) butter or margarine
    ½ cup olive oil
    3 cloves garlic, crushed
    3 tablespoons minced parsley
    2 tablespoons lemon juice
       4 to 6 large, hot, cooked artichokes,
         drained

Peel and devein shrimp; to devein without cutting, slip a thin wooden skewer through the back of each shrimp; then pull it gently up through the back, lifting and pulling out the vein (if present, it can be seen). Repeat along the back in several spots if the vein breaks. If you want to cook the shrimp in their shells, use this same deveining method, penetrating the back through the shell.

Impale 8 to 10 shrimp close together, one on top of another, on 2 thin, wooden, parallel skewers: Put one skewer through the thick section of the shrimp, the other through the tail section to hold the shrimp flat.

Melt butter in a saucepan; then add the olive oil, garlic, and parsley. Heat the sauce just until it bubbles. Remove from heat.

Place skewered shrimp on a rack in a pan; brush generously with garlic sauce. Broil shrimp 4 inches from heat for about 4 minutes or until they turn bright pink. Baste at least once with garlic sauce. Turn and broil about 3 minutes on the remaining side or until shrimp feel firm when pinched; baste once.

Arrange shrimp and hot artichokes on a serving tray. At once, heat garlic sauce to bubbling, add the lemon juice, and pour into individual bowls. Dip artichoke leaves and shrimp into garlic sauce to eat. Makes 4 to 6 servings.

Pearl Rice and Green Pea Salad

In ½ cup olive oil, cook 1 cup short grain rice (such as California pearl) until grains are opaque; add 2½ cups water and 3 chicken bouillon cubes, blending. Bring to boil, cover, and simmer 15 minutes; stir occasionally, until liquid is absorbed and rice is tender. Remove from heat, uncover, and let stand at room temperature. Just before serving, stir in 2 tablespoons minced parsley, 1 package (10 oz.) completely thawed frozen tiny peas, 10 to 12 minced green onions (including part of the tops), and 4 tablespoons freshly squeezed lemon juice. Pass shredded Parmesan cheese to sprinkle over individual portions. Makes 4 to 6 servings.

A Crab Feed

Mixed Green Salad
Messy Crab ·
French Bread   Butter
Strawberries with Hard Sauce

By picking out succulent bits of crab, diners get involved in this menu. Keep hands and clothes reasonably clean by giving them oversized bibs or towels to drape around their necks.

Ask your fish dealer to clean and crack freshly cooked Dungeness crabs. You can prepare the sauce shortly before serving or make it earlier. Then add pieces of crab (bring sauce to simmering if made ahead) and heat briefly.

Messy Crab

    2 large onions, chopped
    4 cloves garlic, minced or mashed
    ½ cup (¼ lb.) butter or margarine
    2 tablespoons all-purpose flour
    3 cups milk
    1 cup whipping cream
      2 to 3 large cooked Dungeness crabs
        (about 2 lbs. each), cleaned and
        well cracked
      Salt and pepper to taste
    1 cup chopped parsley
      Lemon wedges
      Crusty French bread

In a Dutch oven, cook the onion and garlic in the butter until onion is soft. Add the flour and cook, stirring, until flour is golden. Remove pan from heat and gradually stir in the milk and cream. Return pan to heat and bring to simmering,

stirring. Add the crab, cover, and simmer about 10 minutes or until crab is heated through. Season to taste with salt and pepper; stir in the parsley.

Ladle crab and broth into shallow bowls; pass lemons; dunk bread in the broth. Serves 4.

Strawberries with Hard Sauce

In a small bowl, beat 6 tablespoons sweet (unsalted) butter until creamy. Gradually add 1 cup sifted powdered sugar; beat until smooth and fluffy. Stir in 2 tablespoons rum or ¼ teaspoon rum flavoring (refrigerate if made ahead). Serve at room temperature. Hull and slice 1 box strawberries; sweeten to taste with about 2 tablespoons sugar. Serve the sauce and berries each in a small bowl. Spread the sauce on hot waffles or biscuits; then top with berries. Makes about 4 servings.

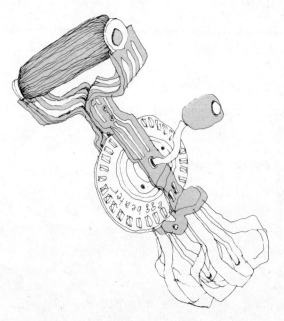

Omelets for a Late Supper

Sesame Omelets

2 or 3 eggs
2 to 3 teaspoons water
¼ teaspoon salt
2 to 3 teaspoons butter or margarine
2 to 3 teaspoons sesame seed
1 tablespoon grated or shredded
   Parmesan cheese

Sesame Omelets

Relish Tray: Italian-Style Pickled
Peppers, Olives, Radishes, Green Onions

Sliced Mortadella or Boiled Ham

Toasted Whole Wheat English Muffins

Cantaloupe Wedges

Omelets are ideal for late-evening entertaining. They require little effort in preparation and serving. And the speed with which you can create an omelet makes it a perfect choice for any hurry-up meal; this variation incorporates some crunchy sesame seeds that toast in the butter before you add the eggs. The omelet recipe makes enough to serve 1. You can make omelets in rapid succession depending on the number of guests.

Arrange the relishes, set out the cold meat (allow about ⅛ lb. for each person), and seed the melon; then toast the muffins while you make the omelets.

For each serving beat eggs, water, and salt with a fork just until whites and yolks are blended. (You can mix all the eggs at once, pouring them a portion at a time into the omelet pan.)

Place butter in a 6 to 7-inch omelet pan over high heat; just as the butter melts enough to coat pan bottom, add the sesame seed. Shake pan to mix seeds as soon as the butter begins to brown lightly, pour in the eggs for 1 omelet all at once. When eggs form an opaque layer over pan bottom, push aside to allow uncooked egg to flow to bottom; continue until all the egg is cooked. Shake pan occasionally to keep omelet free. Sprinkle surface with the Parmesan cheese.

Tilt pan and, with a spatula to guide, fold about ⅓ of the omelet down over the center. Then shake and glide the uncovered edge onto a serving dish; tip remainder of the omelet out and over this edge. Makes 1 omelet.

Fondue Party

Crab Cheese Fondue

Bread Sticks and Crusty Bread Strips

Crisp Raw Vegetables

Almond Peach Custard

This easily assembled menu makes a light but satisfying meal to serve at almost any time of day. (Also consider this fondue and vegetable combination as a party appetizer; it will serve twice as many in that role.)

For dipping up the fondue, offer an assortment of bread sticks and bread, cut in finger-length strips. Choose crusty French bread or a firm dark bread and leave as much crust as possible on each piece. (Or, if you use fondue forks for dunking, cube the bread.)

Choose 3 or 4 raw vegetables such as carrots, celery, cauliflower, jicama, mushrooms, green pepper, turnips, or zucchini. Clean and cut each into one or two bite-sized sticks, slices, or pieces. Allow a dozen or so pieces for each person. Then stir the fondue together just before serving.

You can make the dessert up to a day ahead.

(Continued on next page)

Crab Cheese Fondue

    3 jars (5 oz. each) sharp, pasteurized,
         process cheese spread
       About ½ cup milk or dry Sherry
    2 tablespoons minced green onion
    1 pound crab meat

Combine cheese and the milk in a fondue pot or chafing dish. Place over low direct heat and cook until cheese is melted and bubbly, stirring frequently. Gently stir in onion and crab.

To serve, place fondue pot over low heat. Each person can stir the mixture when dipping pieces of bread or vegetables. If the mixture becomes too thick, add more milk, a few tablespoons at a time. Serves 4 to 6 as a main dish.

Almond Peach Custard

    1 can (1 lb.) water-packed peach
         halves, drained
    1½ cups skim milk, scalded
    2 eggs, beaten
    3 tablespoons sugar
    ½ teaspoon almond extract
    ⅛ teaspoon salt

Place an equal portion of peaches in each of 6 individual ramekins. Blend together scalded skim milk, beaten eggs, sugar, almond extract, and salt. Pour an equal amount into each of the ramekins. Place in a pan of water, half the depth of the custards, and bake in a 350° oven for 25 minutes or until custard is set (shake gently to test). Chill. Makes 6 servings.

Coffee Table Sausage Buffet

Assorted Sausages

Mustard   Horseradish

Browned Potato Puffs

Fresh Spinach Salad

Raisin Bread Party Pudding

If you plan a cook-it-yourself party, have long-handled forks available for grilling the sausages in the fireplace. Serve the tangy, lemon-flavored bread pudding hot from the oven—it can bake while you enjoy the rest of the meal.

Choose an assortment of fully cooked sausages, such as smoked sausage links, garlic frankfurters, or kielbasa, if you just plan to brown them over the fire. Or if you prefer, cook the sausages in the kitchen and serve them on a warm platter ready to eat. Allow 2 or 3 per person. You can assemble the pudding ingredients ahead of time and then fold in the egg whites just before you bake it. Stick it in the oven just before you start serving dinner.

Fresh Spinach Salad

    ¾ pound (about 1 bunch) spinach
       6 to 8 ounces fresh bean sprouts,
         rinsed and drained
    1 can (5 oz.) water chestnuts, drained
         and sliced
    4 green onions, thinly sliced
    ¼ cup each salad oil and white wine
         vinegar
    2 tablespoons catsup
       Salt and pepper
    8 slices bacon, fried and crumbled
    2 hard-cooked eggs, sliced

Remove stems from spinach and discard. Wash leaves well, pat dry, and break into bite-sized pieces. Combine the spinach, bean sprouts, water chestnuts, and onions; cover and refrigerate as long as 4 hours.

Mix together the salad oil, vinegar, catsup, and salt and pepper to taste. Add bacon to spinach mixture, pour dressing over, and mix gently. Garnish with egg slices. Serves 6 to 8.

Raisin Bread Party Pudding

    4 or 5 slices raisin bread
 ¾ cup sugar
1½ teaspoons grated lemon peel
 3 tablespoons lemon juice
 ⅓ cup melted butter or margarine
 3 eggs, separated
 ⅔ cup milk
    Whipped cream (optional)

Cut the raisin bread into ½-inch cubes; you should have 2½ cups. In a large bowl, mix together the bread cubes, ¼ cup of the sugar, lemon peel and juice, and butter. In another bowl, beat egg yolks until thick; stir in milk. Add egg yolk mixture to bread cubes and mix well. You can do this much an hour or so ahead.

Just before baking, beat the egg whites until soft peaks form; gradually add the remaining ½ cup sugar and beat until whites hold stiff peaks. Gently fold egg whites into bread mixture. Turn into a greased 1½-quart shallow baking dish. Bake in a 350° oven for 35 to 40 minutes or until set when touched in the center and richly browned. Serve immediately, topped with whipped cream, if you wish. Makes 6 servings.

Company Scallopini

Pork Scallopini
Broccoli with Broiled Topping
Hot Buttered Noodles
Mixed Green Salad
Chocolate Custard Dessert

Flavorful pork butt, pounded thin, distinguishes this version of scallopini. You can whip up the custard quickly in your blender just before dinner—or make it early in the day if time is short.

Pork Scallopini

1½ pounds pork butt, thinly sliced
    About ½ cup all-purpose flour
    About 1 tablespoon each butter or
      margarine and salad oil
 ½ cup chopped green onion
 1 clove garlic, minced or mashed
 1 teaspoon salt
 ½ teaspoon oregano leaves
 ⅛ teaspoon pepper
 ½ cup Sherry
 ¼ cup water
 ⅓ pound mushrooms, sliced

Pound meat slices thin as possible. Lightly dredge in flour, shaking off excess.

Heat 1 tablespoon each of the butter and salad oil in a frying pan over medium-high heat. Add meat slices, a few at a time, and brown quickly on both sides; remove from pan as browned. Add more butter and salad oil to pan, if needed, to brown remaining meat slices.

Stir in the onion, garlic, salt, oregano, and pepper. Return meat to pan and pour in the Sherry and water. Reduce heat, cover, and simmer 30 minutes, adding water if needed. Add mushrooms to pan, cover and simmer 15 minutes longer or until meat is tender. Makes 4 to 6 servings.

(Continued on next page)

Broccoli with Broiled Topping

1½ to 2 pounds broccoli
    Boiling salted water
½ cup mayonnaise
¼ cup freshly grated Parmesan cheese
2 tablespoons finely chopped parsley
2 teaspoons lemon juice
2 egg whites

Trim off tough ends from broccoli and separate into thin spears; rinse well. Drop the broccoli spears into boiling water and cook, uncovered, until just tender when pierced (about 7 minutes). Drain well, and arrange in a shallow, oven-proof, 1½-quart dish.

Meanwhile, in a small bowl combine the mayonnaise, Parmesan cheese, parsley, and lemon juice. Beat the egg whites until stiff but still moist; fold into the mayonnaise mixture. Spread the topping evenly over the cooked broccoli. Broil 8 to 10 minutes below heat until topping is richly browned (about 5 minutes). Serve immediately. Makes 4 to 6 servings.

Chocolate Custard Dessert

6 egg yolks
1 cup sugar
1 teaspoon vanilla
2 cups milk
4 squares (1 oz. each) unsweetened
    chocolate, cut into quarters
    Chopped nuts or whipped cream for
    garnish

In a blender jar, combine the egg yolks, sugar, and vanilla. Whirl on low speed until mixture is blended; turn off motor and scrape container sides with a rubber spatula. Heat milk and chocolate, stirring (chocolate does not have to melt completely).

Cover blender, turn motor on low speed, remove cover, pour in hot liquid, and blend about 10 seconds or until smooth.

Pour into 6 dessert bowls (about ¾ to 1 cup size); chill until set (1 to 2 hours). To serve, garnish with nuts or whipped cream. Makes 6 servings.

Spicy Brazilian-Style Shrimp

Shrimp and Vegetable Sauté

Brown Rice

Walnut Torte

From Bahia on the east coast of Brazil comes the unusual and colorful entrée for this menu. It is distinguished by a pungent blend of spices that permeates the succulent pink shrimp and lightly cooked vegetables. Let the Walnut Torte bake while you prepare the entrée.

Shrimp and Vegetable Sauté

1 bunch spinach (about ¾ lb.)
¼ cup flaked coconut
3 tablespoons salad oil
1 pound medium-sized (about 32)
    shrimp, shelled and deveined
1 medium-sized onion, chopped
1 clove garlic, minced or mashed
1 package (9 oz.) frozen cut green
    beans, thawed
¼ teaspoon each ground ginger, ground
    cumin seed, ground coriander, and
    paprika
¼ teaspoon crushed red pepper
    Salt and pepper
¼ cup shredded coconut

Discard spinach stems; rinse leaves well, pat dry, and cut into short shreds; set aside. In a large frying pan over medium heat, toast coconut, stirring until golden; lift out and set aside.

To the pan, add 2 tablespoons of the oil and shrimp; sauté until shrimp are pink on all sides and firm throughout (about 5 minutes). With a slotted spoon lift out shrimp. Add remaining oil to the pan; stir in onion and garlic and cook until onion is limp. Stir in green beans, ginger, cumin, coriander, paprika, and red pepper. Cook, stirring, for 3 minutes. Add the spinach, cook 1 minute; then return shrimp and cook just until heated through (about 1 minute longer). Season to taste with salt and pepper; sprinkle with coconut. Makes 4 servings.

Walnut Torte

3 eggs
1 cup sugar
1 cup crushed graham cracker crumbs
½ cup chopped walnuts
   Currant jelly
   Whipped cream

Beat eggs until thick and lemon colored. Add sugar, crumbs, and nuts; mix well. Pour batter into a greased and floured 9-inch cake pan. Bake in a 350° oven for 25 minutes or until a wooden pick inserted in the center comes out clean. Cool in pan. Turn onto a serving dish and spread cake with a thin layer of jelly; top with whipped cream. Cut in wedges. Makes 8 servings.

Speedy Stroganoff

Meatball Stroganoff
Fluffy White Rice or Buttered Noodles
Chocolate Chip Ice Cream
Coffee or Tea

This ground beef stroganoff might become a favorite spur-of-the-moment company dish to serve over rice or buttered noodles.

Meatball Stroganoff

½ pound mushrooms
4 tablespoons butter or margarine
1 medium-sized onion, finely chopped
2 pounds lean ground beef
1 teaspoon salt
½ teaspoon crumbled tarragon leaves
¼ teaspoon each pepper and sweet
      basil leaves
2 tablespoons all-purpose flour
⅓ cup canned tomato paste
1 can (10 oz.) condensed beef
      consommé
2 teaspoons Worcestershire
1 tablespoon vinegar
1 cup sour cream

Slice mushrooms and sauté in a large frying pan in 2 tablespoons of the butter; turn out of pan and set aside. Add the remaining 2 tablespoons butter to pan and sauté onion until golden; push to sides of pan. Quickly shape meat into bite-sized balls and drop into pan; sauté, shaking pan to turn, until browned. Sprinkle with salt, tarragon, pepper, basil, and flour. Add tomato paste, consommé, Worcestershire, and vinegar; cover and simmer 10 minutes. Add mushrooms to meat and remove from heat. Stir in sour cream. Makes 4 to 6 servings.

An Oriental Dinner

Tomato Juice   Wheat Crackers
Crab Foo Yung
Skillet Snow Peas with Celery
Pears Flambé

Fresh bean sprouts give tender crispness to these Crab Foo Yung patties. Carry out the Oriental theme by serving Chinese edible pod peas with celery as a side dish. Hold the patties on a warming tray while you quickly cook the peas.

You may wish to cook the dessert at the table in a chafing dish.

Crab Foo Yung

    4 eggs, well beaten
    1 package (7½ oz.) fresh bean sprouts,
        washed and drained
    ⅓ cup (about 6) thinly sliced green onions
    1 cup (about 8 oz.) flaked, cooked
        crabmeat
    ½ teaspoon salt
    ⅛ teaspoon each pepper and garlic
        powder
    2 tablespoons salad oil
        Foo Yung Sauce (recipe follows)

Combine eggs, bean sprouts, onions, crabmeat, salt (omit the salt if using canned crabmeat), pepper, and garlic powder, mixing lightly. Heat the oil in a large frying pan, using just enough to coat pan; add remaining oil as needed. Using about ¼ cup of the mixture for each, fry egg-crabmeat patties as you would pancakes, turning once. Cook until set and lightly browned. Remove to a warming platter and serve with Foo Yung Sauce. Makes 4 servings.

Foo Yung Sauce. In a pan, combine 1 teaspoon cornstarch, 1 teaspoon sugar, 2 teaspoons soy sauce, and 1 teaspoon vinegar; stir in ½ cup regular-strength chicken broth or 1 chicken bouillon cube dissolved in ½ cup water. Cook over low heat until thickened.

Skillet Snow Peas with Celery

    ½ cup sliced green onion tops
    4 stalks celery, cut in thin slanting
        slices
    1 pound edible pod peas, ends and
        strings removed
    1 tablespoon cornstarch
    ½ teaspoon salt
    1 teaspoon sugar
    1 tablespoon soy sauce
    ½ cup water
    2 tablespoons salad oil

Prepare the green onion, celery, and pod peas and have within reach of your range. In a small bowl, stir together the cornstarch, salt, sugar, soy sauce, and water; set aside. In a large frying pan or wok, heat salad oil over high heat. Add onion, celery, and peas; stir-fry 2 minutes. Add cornstarch mixture to vegetables and cook, stirring, until peas are barely tender (about 2 minutes more). Serve immediately. Makes about 4 servings.

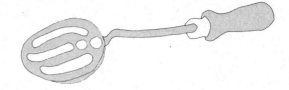

Pears Flambé

    4 tablespoons butter or margarine
    3 whole firm Anjou or Bosc pears,
        peeled, cored, and sliced
        Lemon juice
    3 or 4 tablespoons sugar (or to taste)
    ¼ cup rum, brandy, or Cointreau,
        slightly heated
        Ice cream or whipping cream (optional)

Melt butter in a frying pan or chafing dish over medium to high heat and add pear slices. (If you peel the pears ahead, sprinkle with lemon juice to keep them from turning brown.) Sprinkle with sugar and heat, shaking the pan and stirring gently until pear slices are well coated with butter. Pour the rum, brandy, or Cointreau over them and ignite. Serve immediately. (The pears should not be overcooked.) Serve over ice cream or with whipping cream poured over the fruit, if you wish. Makes 4 servings.

Light Patio Supper

Pineapple Chicken Salad
Toasted English Muffins
Iced Tea
Quick Blueberry Crisp

Assemble this crunchy Pineapple Chicken Salad in the morning. It is served on a pineapple ring, sprinkled with cheese, and slipped under the broiler briefly to melt the cheese. Serve it atop a toasted muffin half like a big open-face sandwich or serve the broiled salad with the toasted muffins on the side.

You can use leftover cooked chicken or turkey for the salad. Or simply simmer 1½ pounds chicken breast in a small amount of salted water until meat is no longer pink throughout (about 15 minutes). When cool, discard skin and bones; cut or tear meat into thin pieces.

Pineapple Chicken Salad

    1 to 2 cups cooked chicken or
       turkey, in bite-sized pieces
    ½ cup mayonnaise
    1 teaspoon Dijon mustard
    ½ cup thinly sliced celery
    ¼ cup chopped green onion
       Salt and pepper to taste
    ⅓ cup toasted sliced almonds
    1 can (about 8 oz.) sliced pineapple,
       drained, or 4 thin slices fresh
       pineapple, peeled and cored
       About ½ cup shredded Cheddar
       cheese
    2 English muffins, split, toasted, and
       buttered

Stir together the chicken, mayonnaise, mustard, celery, and green onion. Season to taste with salt and pepper. Cover and chill until serving.

To serve, gently stir in almonds. Arrange 4 slices of pineapple on a broiler pan; top each with an equal amount of chicken salad and sprinkle with cheese. Broil about 4 inches from the heat just until cheese melts. With a wide spatula, lift onto muffin halves or directly onto plates. Makes 4 servings.

Quick Blueberry Crisp

    2 cans (15 oz. each) blueberries,
       drained (reserve syrup for
       pancakes or dessert sauce)
    1 tablespoon lemon juice
    ⅔ cup firmly packed brown sugar
    ½ cup all-purpose flour, unsifted
    ¼ teaspoon salt
    ¼ teaspoon ground nutmeg
    ¼ cup butter or margarine, at room
       temperature
       Ice cream of your choice

Place blueberries in a buttered, shallow casserole (about 6½ by 9½ inches); sprinkle with lemon juice. Mix brown sugar, flour, salt, and nutmeg; cut in butter or margarine until crumbly. Cover berries with brown sugar mixture. Bake in a 400° oven for 15 to 20 minutes or until bubbly. Serve warm with ice cream over top. Makes 4 to 6 servings.

Make-Ahead Dinners

Transportable Menu

Carrot Sticks   Bread Sticks

Bean and Tuna Salad

Italian Sausage Soup with
Grated Parmesan Cheese

Crisp Apples   Italian Cookies

Pack this soup to take with you on an outing or have it ready and waiting in the refrigerator to reheat and quickly assemble when you return.

You can make the soup a day ahead; then cool and refrigerate it until it's time to leave. On the day before, you might also grate the cheese and peel and cut the carrots; pack in separate containers. Mix together the beans and dressing and refrigerate in a covered container. Open and drain the tuna, but leave it in the can and enclose in a plastic bag; chill.

In the morning, either reheat the soup and pour it into vacuum bottles to keep hot or bring the cold soup in covered containers to heat up at your destination.

Bean and Tuna Salad

Mix together 2 cans (about 1 lb. *each*) white kidney beans or garbanzo beans (rinsed and drained), ½ cup Italian dressing, 2 tablespoons each dehydrated sweet red pepper flakes and parsley flakes. Cover and chill until ready to serve. To serve, unmold 1 can (7 oz.) chunk-style tuna (drained) in the center of a plate. Arrange the bean mixture around it. Makes 6 servings.

Italian Sausage Soup

1½ pounds mild Italian sausage, cut in
    ½-inch lengths
2 cloves garlic, minced or mashed
2 large onions, chopped
1 large can (about 28 oz.) pear-
    shaped tomatoes
3 cans (about 14 oz. each) regular-
    strength beef broth
1½ cups dry red wine or water
½ teaspoon crumbled basil leaves
3 tablespoons chopped parsley
1 medium-sized green pepper, chopped
2 medium-sized zucchini, sliced ¼ inch
    thick
3 cups uncooked bow-tie noodles
    Grated Parmesan cheese

In a 5-quart or larger Dutch oven, cook the sausages over medium heat until lightly browned. Drain off and discard any fat. Add the garlic and onions; cook, stirring, until limp. Stir in the tomatoes (including the liquid), breaking them into pieces with a spoon. Then add the broth, wine or water, and basil. Simmer, uncovered, for 30 minutes. Cool; then chill. Later, remove and discard the fat.

If you plan to reheat the soup at your destination, pack the parsley, pepper, zucchini, and noodles in separate bags and carry them along. When reheating the soup, add them and simmer, covered, for about 25 minutes or until noodles are tender. Or if you take the soup in vacuum bottles, reheat the soup to simmering just before you leave and add the parsley, pepper, zucchini, and noodles and cook as directed above.

To serve, ladle or pour into bowls. Pass grated cheese to sprinkle over individual servings. Makes 6 servings.

Company Casserole Dinner

Hot Vegetable Broth
Broccoli Spears with Italian Dressing
Cheddar Seafood Casserole
Buttered Rice
Pineapple Sherbet

This festive company dinner for 8 is planned around a make-ahead casserole filled with shrimp, oysters, and crab.

You might offer small mugs of the hot vegetable broth in the living room while the casserole heats in the oven. Fill mugs with hot cocktail vegetable juice (for 8 servings you'll need a 46-oz. can). To each serving add a squeeze of lemon juice, a dollop of sour cream, and a sprinkling of dill weed.

Just before serving, moisten cold cooked broccoli spears (you'll need 2½ to 3 lbs.) with prepared Italian-style dressing and top with sliced green onion.

Cheddar Seafood Casserole

7 tablespoons butter or margarine
4 tablespoons all-purpose flour
1½ cups milk
½ teaspoon salt
¼ teaspoon thyme leaves
⅛ teaspoon each pepper and dry
    mustard
2½ cups shredded medium or sharp
    Cheddar cheese
2 egg yolks, slightly beaten
½ pound mushrooms, sliced
1 jar (10 oz.) Pacific oysters, cut in
    bite-sized pieces
1 pound crab meat
1 pound medium-sized shrimp (about
    32), cooked, shelled, and deveined
1 tablespoon lemon juice

In a 3-quart saucepan, melt 4 tablespoons of the butter; stir in the flour and cook until bubbly.

(Continued on next page)

Remove from heat and gradually add the milk; cook, stirring until thickened. Add the salt, thyme, pepper, mustard, and 2 cups of the cheese; stir until cheese is melted. Add the egg yolks and cook over low heat 3 minutes longer; set aside.

Meanwhile, melt the remaining 3 tablespoons butter in a wide frying pan over medium heat; add the mushrooms and sauté until lightly browned and the liquid is evaporated. Add mushrooms and butter to the cheese sauce. To the frying pan, add oysters and their liquid; simmer until the edges begin to curl. Drain off liquid and stir oysters into sauce, along with the crab meat, shrimp, and lemon juice. Turn mixture into a 2-quart casserole; sprinkle remaining cheese evenly over top. Cover and chill if made ahead. Before serving, bake, uncovered, in a 375° oven until cheese is melted and mixture is heated through, 20 to 25 minutes (30 minutes if refrigerated). Makes 8 servings.

Hamburgers Ahead

Beef and Cheese Buns

French Fries

Crisp Relish Tray

Coffee Cream Sundaes

You can assemble these hearty sandwiches the day before—then they are ready to heat and serve. To feed a hungry crowd, just double or triple the recipe accordingly. Along with the beef buns, slip frozen French fries into the oven (following package directions).

Make the coffee syrup for the sundaes ahead or while the buns are in the oven.

Beef and Cheese Buns

1 pound lean ground beef
1 tablespoon chopped green onion
¾ teaspoon salt
¼ teaspoon pepper
2 tablespoons catsup
Cheese Topping (recipe follows)
4 round hamburger buns, split and
   lightly buttered

Combine the ground beef, onion, salt, pepper, and catsup; mix well and shape into 4 patties. Place on the rack of a broiler pan; broil about 4 inches from heat until browned on both sides and done to your liking (4 to 5 minutes total for medium). Let cool while you prepare the cheese topping.

Place each meaty patty on a bun half; top with about ¼ of the cheese topping and remaining bun half. Wrap each bun tightly in foil; refrigerate as long as overnight.

To heat, place wrapped buns in a 350° oven for about 30 minutes or until meat is heated through. Serves 4.

Cheese Topping. Combine 1 cup shredded sharp Cheddar cheese, 2 tablespoons soft butter, 1½ teaspoons catsup, ½ teaspoon prepared mustard, and 1 tablespoon finely chopped green onion.

Coffee Cream Sundaes

1 cup each firmly packed brown sugar
   and strong coffee
¼ teaspoon vanilla
1 tablespoon brandy
   Coffee ice cream
   Whipped cream
   Toasted almonds

In a saucepan combine the brown sugar and coffee; bring to boiling and boil, uncovered, until thickened (about 10 minutes). Remove from heat. Add the vanilla and brandy; cool. Serve syrup over scoops of coffee ice cream. Top each serving with a dollop of whipped cream and sprinkle with toasted almonds. Makes enough syrup for 4 servings.

Individual Molded Salads

Corned Beef on Cabbage Salad
Crescent Rolls
Apple Almond Squares

A molded main dish salad is a boon to the hostess who's looking for a supper menu with a minimum of last-minute preparation. You can make these individual salads early in the day (or a day ahead) using leftover corned beef or canned corned beef. Make the dessert ahead or shortly before dinner to serve warm.

Corned Beef on Cabbage Salad

1 envelope unflavored gelatin
1 can (about 14 oz.) regular-strength beef broth
½ cup each mayonnaise and sour cream
2 tablespoons prepared mustard
1 tablespoon each horseradish and vinegar
2 cans (12 oz. each) corned beef, finely diced (or 3 cups diced cooked corned beef)
1 can (about 1 lb.) small whole potatoes, cut in ¼-inch dice (about 2 cups)
2 hard-cooked eggs, chopped
½ cup finely chopped celery
¼ cup finely chopped green onion
Cabbage Salad with Mustard Dressing (recipe follows)

Soften gelatin in broth; set over simmering water and heat, stirring, to dissolve gelatin; cool. Stir in mayonnaise, sour cream, mustard, horseradish, and vinegar; refrigerate until slightly thickened, stirring occasionally. Combine corned beef, potatoes, eggs, celery, and green onion; stir into slightly thickened gelatin mixture. Spoon into 6 or 7 molds (1 cup size); chill until set (about 2 hours).

Unmold each serving on a bed of cabbage salad. Garnish the plates with dill pickle wedges and cherry tomatoes, if you wish. Makes 6 servings.

Cabbage Salad with Mustard Dressing. Finely shred enough cabbage to make about 6 cups. Mix in ½ cup each chopped parsley and chopped green onions. For the dressing, combine ⅓ cup each mayonnaise and sour cream, 2 tablespoons each prepared mustard and lemon juice, ¼ teaspoon celery seed, ⅛ teaspoon salt. Mix dressing into cabbage.

Apple Almond Squares

½ cup (¼ lb.) butter or margarine
1 cup sugar
3 eggs
2 cups graham cracker crumbs
½ cup all-purpose flour, unsifted
2 teaspoons baking powder
½ teaspoon each salt and ground allspice
2 teaspoons ground cinnamon
1 cup milk
2 cups peeled and finely chopped tart apple
¾ cup chopped blanched almonds
Powdered sugar

In a large bowl, beat together the butter and sugar until creamy; add eggs one at a time, beating well after each addition. Stir together the crumbs, flour, baking powder, salt, allspice, and cinnamon; stir into the butter mixture along with the milk until blended. Stir in the apple and almonds until evenly distributed.

Spread batter in a well-greased and flour-dusted 9 by 13-inch baking pan. Bake in a 350° oven for 35 minutes or until a wooden pick inserted in the center comes out clean.

Dust with powdered sugar just before serving; offer warm or at room temperature. Makes 10 to 12 servings.

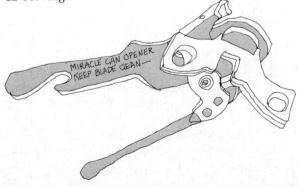

MIRACLE CAN OPENER
KEEP BLADE CLEAN—

Crêpes from the Freezer

Chicken and Artichoke Crêpes

Wilted Lettuce and Tomatoes

Chocolate Tortini

You can freeze the filled crêpes individually; then bake—without thawing—as many as you'll need. To freeze, place filled crêpes seam-side-down (without touching) on greased baking sheets. Freeze the crêpes uncovered; then package them airtight. For best flavor, use within 2 weeks.

The salad is a switch from the usual bacon-vinegar dressed wilted salad; it "wilts" from a brown butter and sesame seed dressing.

Make and freeze the Chocolate Tortini a day ahead. Seal in foil if made more than a day ahead.

Chicken and Artichoke Crêpes

    12 to 16 crêpes (directions follow)
5 tablespoons butter or margarine
1 small onion, chopped
¼ pound mushrooms, sliced
3 tablespoons all-purpose flour
⅔ cup regular-strength chicken broth
½ cup half-and-half (light cream)
2 cups cooked chicken or turkey, torn
    into bite-sized pieces
1 package (8 oz.) frozen artichoke
    hearts, thawed, drained, and cut
    into thirds
⅓ cup grated Parmesan cheese
¼ teaspoon crushed rosemary leaves
½ teaspoon salt
    Shredded Swiss cheese

Prepare crêpes or bring to room temperature if refrigerated. Melt 2 tablespoons of the butter in a frying pan; add onion and mushrooms. Cook, stirring, until mushrooms are limp. Stir in remaining butter until melted; add flour and cook, stirring, until bubbly. Gradually stir in broth and cream; cook, stirring, until it boils and thickens. Remove from heat; stir in chicken, artichokes, Parmesan, rosemary, salt; cool.

Divide filling equally between crêpes, spooning it down the center of each; roll to enclose. If made ahead, freeze as directed above.

To serve, arrange desired number of fresh or frozen crêpes in a shallow casserole or in individual ramekins. Cover with foil and bake in a 375° oven for 20 minutes (or 35 to 40 minutes if frozen). Sprinkle crêpes with Swiss cheese (use ½ cup for full recipe). Bake, uncovered, until cheese melts. Serves 6 to 8.

To make the crepes, combine 1 cup milk and 3 eggs in a blender; add ⅔ cup unsifted all-purpose flour. Cover and whirl until smooth (or blend eggs and milk with a wire whip; then add flour and mix until smooth).

Place a 6 or 7-inch crêpe pan (or other flat-bottomed frying pan of this size) on medium heat. When pan is hot, add ¼ teaspoon butter and swirl to coat surface. At once, pour in 1½ or 2 tablespoons batter, quickly tilting pan so batter flows over the entire flat surface. (Don't worry if there are a few little holes.) Cook until the surface appears dry and the edge is lightly browned. With a spatula, turn and brown the other side. Turn out of pan onto a plate. Repeat procedure for each crêpe, stacking them.

If you do not use the baked crêpes within a few hours, cool, package airtight, and refrigerate for as long as a week. Let crêpes come to room temperature before separating; they tear if cold. Makes 12 to 16 crêpes.

Wilted Lettuce and Tomatoes

Break enough tender leaves of romaine or butter lettuce into a bowl to make 4 cups. Add 3 tomatoes, peeled and cut in thin wedges. Sprinkle with salt and freshly ground pepper.

In a saucepan, slowly heat ½ cup (¼ lb.) butter with 3 tablespoons sesame seed until butter is lightly browned. Pour hot butter over lettuce and tomatoes and quickly cover. After 2 minutes remove cover, mix, and serve. Make 4 generous servings.

Chocolate Tortini

Crush enough chocolate-flavored wafer cookies to make ½ cup coarse crumbs. Place 2 teaspoons crumbs in each of 6 paper cupcake pan liners; top with a scoop of chocolate or chocolate ripple ice cream. Fill in around ice cream with remaining crumbs, sprinkling a few crumbs over the top. Freeze until ready to serve (seal in foil if made more than a day ahead). When you serve, top each serving with a small dollop marshmallow sauce and a maraschino cherry with a stem. Serves 6.

Chilled Salmon with Lomi Lomi

Hot Creamed Vegetable Soup

Chilled Poached Salmon (or Turbot) Fillets

Lomi Lomi Relish

Warm Rolls   Butter

Frosty Lemon Torte

In Hawaii, *lomi lomi* in its basic form consists of salted smoked salmon combined with chopped tomatoes and onions. Here we suggest poached salmon or turbot fillets served chilled with a lomi lomi-style vegetable relish to accompany each serving.

Early in the day, poach the fish and prepare the relish to allow for ample chilling time. If you use the mild-flavored turbot fillets, you might want to use the upper level of green chiles for a hotter relish.

You can prepare your favorite creamed green vegetable soup, such as asparagus, zucchini, or split pea; or simply heat 2 cans (about 11 oz. *each*) condensed soup according to the directions on the can.

Freeze the Frosty Lemon Torte early in the morning or the night before.

Chilled Poached Salmon (or Turbot) with Lomi Lomi Relish

2 cups water
1 small onion, sliced
3 whole black peppers
1 small bay leaf
1½ teaspoons lemon juice
½ teaspoon salt
About 2 pounds salmon fillet or Greenland turbot fillets, thawed
Butter lettuce leaves, washed and chilled
Lomi Lomi Relish (recipe follows)
Lemon wedges

In a wide frying pan, combine the water, onion, pepper, bay leaf, lemon juice, and salt. Bring to boiling, cover, and simmer about 10 minutes. Cut fish into serving-sized pieces and set in pan. Cover and simmer gently until fish flakes when tested with a fork (about 10 to 12 minutes for salmon, 5 for turbot). With a spatula, remove fish; cover and chill.

Serve fish pieces on lettuce; mound relish to one side of fish. Garnish with lemon wedges. Serves 4 to 6.

Lomi Lomi Relish. Combine in a bowl, 2 medium-sized tomatoes (chopped), 1 large green pepper (seeded and chopped), ½ cup thinly sliced green onion, 1 small onion (chopped), 2 to 3 tablespoons diced canned California green chiles, 2 tablespoons lemon juice, and 1 teaspoon salt. Cover and chill several hours.

Frosty Lemon Torte

1 cup crushed coconut macaroon cooky crumbs
2 tablespoons melted butter or margarine
2 eggs, separated
⅔ cup sugar
1 teaspoon grated lemon peel
⅓ cup lemon juice
Dash salt
⅔ cup each non-fat dry milk and water

Stir together the cooky crumbs and butter. Lightly press about ¾ of the crumbs in the bottom of a 9-inch cake pan with a removable bottom.

With an electric mixer, beat the egg yolks until foamy; then gradually add ½ cup of the sugar and beat until thick and lemon colored. Blend in lemon peel, lemon juice, and salt.

In another bowl, combine the egg whites, dry milk, water, and remaining sugar. Beat on highest speed until stiff peaks form (about 5 minutes). Add yolk mixture and, with mixer on lowest speed, beat just until blended. Pour into prepared pan and sprinkle remaining crumbs over top. Cover and freeze until firm (at least 6 hours or overnight). Remove from freezer 10 minutes before serving. Makes 8 servings.

Mexican Burrito Supper

Mixed Green Salad
Spicy Meat-Filled Burritos
Papaya Halves and Lime Wedges
Sangria or Fruit Punch

A spicy filling made from a leftover beef or pork roast (or from chicken or turkey) combines with warm flour tortillas to make these Mexican burritos. Much of this meal can be made ahead or quickly assembled just before serving.

Wash and chill the lettuce for your favorite green salad. Prepare the relish, meat filling, and cheese for the burritos and chill. Spoon the guacamole and sour cream into their individual serving dishes; cover and refrigerate. Thoroughly chill the papaya and beverage.

Shortly before serving, reheat the meat filling and beans, warm the tortillas for burritos, and mix the salad.

Assemble the makings and arrange them on the table. Your guests will stuff the tortillas with any combination they desire.

Spicy Meat-Filled Burritos

Tomato and Chile Relish (recipe follows)
Spicy Meat Filling (recipe follows)
About 1½ to 2 dozen flour tortillas
1 can (1 lb. 13 oz.) refried beans
About 3 cups shredded jack cheese (about 8 oz.)
2 cans (about 8 oz. each) frozen guacamole, thawed
About 1 cup sour cream

Prepare the Tomato and Chile Relish and chill. Cook the meat filling; reheat if made ahead. While the filling cooks (or reheats), stack the tortillas and wrap tightly in foil. Place in a 350° oven for 15 minutes or until they're warm and soft. Follow directions on the can for heating the refried beans.

To serve, place relish, meat filling, beans, cheese, guacamole, and sour cream in individual bowls. Serve tortillas in a towel-lined basket. Let guests make their own burritos by choosing various foods to roll up in the tortilla, then topping with a spoonful of guacamole and sour cream. Makes 6 to 8 servings.

Tomato and Chile Relish. Seed and finely chop 3 medium-sized tomatoes to make 3 cups. Stir in

1 cup finely chopped green onions (tops included), 2 to 4 tablespoons finely chopped canned California green chiles (seeds and pith removed), and ½ teaspoon each ground coriander and salt. Cover and chill until ready to serve. Drain off excess liquid before serving. Makes about 3 cups.

Spicy Meat Filling. Heat 2 tablespoons oil in a wide frying pan over medium heat. Add 1 large onion (finely chopped) and 2 cloves garlic (minced or mashed). Cook, stirring, until limp. Stir in 4 cups finely diced cooked meat (beef or pork roast, chicken or turkey), 1 can (10 oz.) red chile sauce, 1 teaspoon salt, ½ teaspoon each ground cinnamon and cumin, and 2 to 4 tablespoons chopped canned California green chiles (seeds and pith removed) to taste. Simmer, uncovered, for about 5 minutes. Makes about 5 cups.

No-Work Week-End Dinner

Zucchini Pork Bake
Tossed Green Salad
Parkerhouse Rolls   Butter
Cranberry Chiffon Pie

You assemble the Zucchini Pork Bake and the Cranberry Chiffon Pie ahead for this menu. Pop the casserole into the oven about 45 minutes before serving—then relax.

Zucchini Pork Bake

1 pound lean ground pork
½ teaspoon garlic salt
¼ cup fine dry bread crumbs
3 tablespoons grated Parmesan cheese
1 cup sour cream
6 zucchini, each about 5 inches long
    Salt and pepper
6 ounces sliced mozzarella cheese

In a frying pan over medium heat, cook the pork, stirring, until meat has lost all pinkness. Drain fat; then stir in the garlic salt, crumbs, 2 tablespoons of the Parmesan cheese, and sour cream. Set aside.

Cut zucchini in thin lengthwise slices; sprinkle lightly with salt and pepper. In a greased, shallow, 2-quart baking dish, arrange about half of the zucchini slices; spoon pork mixture evenly over top, and cover with the remaining zucchini slices. (Cover and chill if made ahead.)

Bake, covered, in a 350° oven for 35 minutes (45 minutes if chilled); uncover, arrange mozzarella cheese over top and sprinkle evenly with the remaining Parmesan cheese. Bake, uncovered, for 10 minutes longer or until cheese is golden. Serves 4 to 6.

Cranberry Chiffon Pie

1 envelope unflavored gelatin
¼ cup cold water
2 cups cranberries
½ medium-sized orange, peeled
1 cup sugar
2 egg whites
¼ teaspoon salt
1 teaspoon vanilla
1 cup whipping cream
1 baked 9-inch pie shell

(Continued on next page)

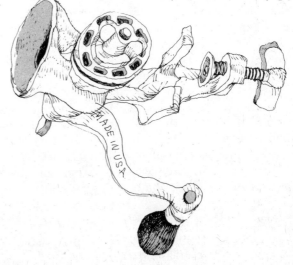

Stir gelatin into cold water; set aside for about 5 minutes to soften. Then stir over hot water until dissolved. Place the cranberries and orange in a blender container; cover and whirl until finely chopped (or put the fruits through a food chopper using a medium blade). Stir in ¾ cup of the sugar and the dissolved gelatin. Cover and chill until syrupy.

Beat the egg whites and salt until soft peaks form; then beat in the remaining ¼ cup sugar. Fold into the cranberry mixture with the vanilla. Whip about ¾ cup of the cream. Fold into cranberry mixture and pour into the baked crust. Chill until set (at least 4 hours or as long as overnight). Before serving, whip the remaining cream to garnish top. Makes 6 servings.

Elegant Casserole Dinner

Butter Lettuce Salad with Avocado and Pine Nuts

Chicken and Artichoke Casserole With Mushrooms

Butter-Glazed Carrots

Apple Cheesecake

Most of the work for this meal—centered around an elegant casserole of chicken, artichoke hearts, and mushrooms—can be completed long before you plan to serve.

Prepare the elements of the casserole early in the day and refrigerate until time to heat and serve. You can also start the carrots well before the meal, if you like. Drain hot, cooked carrots and immerse in ice water to cool quickly; then drain and refrigerate, covered. At serving time lightly brown carrots in melted butter and sprinkle with minced parsley.

For the salad, have butter lettuce washed, dry, and crisped. You could also toast the pine nuts in advance by stirring them in a greased frying pan over medium heat until golden. Before serving, slice avocado into the salad, lightly mix salad with bottled oil and vinegar dressing (or make your own dressing), and sprinkle pine nuts over the top.

Make the cheesecake early in the day so it will have ample time to chill.

Chicken and Artichoke Casserole with Mushrooms

    1 can (about 14 oz.) regular-strength
      chicken broth
2½ to 3 pounds chicken breasts
      (about 4 large whole breasts)
    1 can (14 oz.) artichoke hearts,
      drained
    6 tablespoons butter or margarine
    ¼ cup all-purpose flour
    ¼ teaspoon salt
    ⅛ teaspoon pepper
    ¾ cup half-and-half (light cream)
    ½ cup grated Parmesan cheese
    2 tablespoons Sherry (optional)
    ½ teaspoon rosemary leaves, crushed
    ¼ pound mushrooms, sliced

In a frying pan with a lid or a Dutch oven, bring chicken broth to simmering over medium heat. Place chicken breasts in a single layer, cover, and poach until meat is tender when pierced with a fork (about 15 minutes). Lift chicken from broth; cool. Then remove skin and pull bones from chicken; reserve ¾ cup of the broth for sauce. (Save remaining for another use such as soups or broth stews.) In a shallow casserole (about 8 by 12 inches), arrange chicken breast pieces, slightly overlapping; distribute drained artichoke hearts in casserole. Cover and refrigerate.

In a saucepan over medium heat, melt 4 tablespoons of the butter; stir in flour, salt, and pepper until smoothly blended. Gradually stir in the ¾ cup of the chicken broth and the half-and-half. Cook, stirring, until mixture boils and is thickened. Stir in Parmesan cheese, Sherry, and rosemary until cheese is melted and mixture is blended. Cover and refrigerate.

In a frying pan over medium heat, melt remaining 2 tablespoons butter. Add mushrooms and sauté until golden. Transfer mushrooms to a small dish; cover and refrigerate.

Shortly before serving, stir sauce over low heat until it liquefies; then pour over chicken and artichoke hearts so that artichoke hearts are well covered. Distribute mushrooms down the center of the casserole. Bake, uncovered, in a 325° oven for 30 minutes or until heated through. Makes 6 to 8 servings.

Apple Cheesecake

  1 cup all-purpose flour, unsifted
  3 tablespoons powdered sugar
  ½ cup (¼ lb.) butter or margarine
  2 large Golden Delicious apples
  2 tablespoons sugar
  ¼ cup currants
  1 large package (8 oz.) cream
     cheese, soften
  ¾ cup sugar
  1 teaspoon grated lemon peel
  1 tablespoon lemon juice
  2 eggs

For the pastry, combine flour and powdered sugar. Cut in the butter until mixture resembles cornmeal. With your fingers, press pastry over bottom and sides of an 11-inch flan pan or a 9 or 10-inch regular pie pan.

Halve, peel, and core the apples; then cut in ¼-inch slices. Arrange slices in pan, overlapping slightly. Sprinkle with the 2 tablespoons sugar and the currants.

In the small bowl of an electric mixer, combine the cream cheese, ¾ cup sugar, lemon peel, lemon juice, and eggs. Beat until smooth; then pour evenly over apples. Bake in a 350° oven about 30 minutes or until cheese mixture is just set and very lightly browned around the edge. Serves 8.

Syrian Salad Supper

Hot Clam-and-Tomato Juice

Tabouli

Cold Meat Platter

Hot Buttered Egg Bread

Fruit Platter with Strawberry Ice Cream

Tabouli, a Syrian marinated barley salad served with cold meats, makes a fascinating entrée. It's best if made a day in advance so the mint and lemon dressing can permeate thoroughly.

For ease, purchase the cold meats from a delicatessen. Or, if you prefer, cook and chill a smoked beef tongue (the leftovers make fine sandwiches) and roast a beef cut, such as a sirloin tip, cross-rib, or rolled rib, to serve cold.

You can pre-scoop and refreeze the ice cream balls ahead, too. Just beforehand, heat the canned juice, butter a loaf of egg bread and warm it, and cut the fresh fruit for dessert.

Hot Clam-and-Tomato Juice

Heat 2 cans (16 oz. each) clam-and-tomato juice and serve in mugs with a thin slice of lime floating on each. Makes 8 servings.

(Continued on next page)

Tabouli

3 cups water
1½ teaspoons salt
1¼ cups pearl barley
⅓ cup lemon juice
½ cup olive oil
⅛ teaspoon pepper
3 green onions
1¼ cups finely chopped parsley
¼ cup chopped mint leaves
1 head romaine
1 cucumber
About 1 cup cherry tomatoes

Bring the water and 1 teaspoon of the salt to a boil in a large saucepan, add barley, cover, and simmer 35 minutes or until barley is puffed and almost tender (at this point it will have a chewy texture). Remove from heat. Cool.

For a dressing, mix together the lemon juice, oil, the remaining ½ teaspoon salt, and pepper. Pour over barley and fluff with a fork. Chill. Chop the green onions finely (using both white and green parts) and add to the barley along with parsley and mint. Cover and chill.

To serve, cover a large round platter (preferably one with a slight rim) with the center romaine leaves. Mound barley salad in a cone shape on top of the leaves. Peel and slice cucumber and halve cherry tomatoes, arranging them around the base of the salad. Makes 6 servings.

Cold Meat Platter

Buy a selection of ½ pound each smoked beef tongue, corned beef, and boiled ham or a sausage such as mortadella or a gallantine. (Or select from cold meats you have on hand.) Arrange the meats on a board, either folding them in half or rolling them, if possible. Cover and chill until serving time. Makes enough for 6 servings.

Fruit Platter with Strawberry Ice Cream

Halve 3 small cantaloupe and scoop out the seeds. Place melons on a serving board with small bowls of strawberries (about 1½ cups) and peeled and sliced peaches (about 2). Place small scoops of strawberry ice cream (about 1 quart) in another bowl. Let diners use the melon halves as fruit bowls to fill with the berries, peaches, and ice cream. Makes 6 servings.

Italian Pasta

Fettucini Verde
Browned Italian Sausages
Fresh Citrus Salad Plate

Vegetable noodles coated with a creamy green onion and cheese sauce distinguish this version of fettucini.

Several hours in advance, cut the peel and white membrane off 3 large oranges and 1 white grapefruit. Slice fruit thinly crosswise or cut out segments; marinate in ½ cup of your favorite oil and vinegar dressing. Drain citrus briefly and arrange on a lettuce-lined salad plate to serve.

You can precook the sausages and assemble most of the ingredients for the fettucini ahead. Also arrange the items you'll need at the table. Just before serving, cook the noodles while sausages are browning; then bring pasta to the table for finishing touches.

Fettucini Verde

1 cup chopped green onion (including
  some of the tops)
2 cloves garlic, minced or mashed
6 tablespoons butter or margarine
3 to 4 cups hot cooked, drained
  vegetable noodles
1 cup whipping cream
  About 2 cups grated Parmesan
  cheese
  Salt and pepper
  Freshly grated or ground nutmeg

Cook green onion and garlic in the butter or margarine until onion is limp; transfer to a small container to bring to the table and keep warm.

Just before serving, place the hot, cooked noodles and the cream in an attractive frying pan or other serving dish that can be used over direct heat. Stir the mixture over high heat until the cream reaches boiling point; then immediately bring it to the table along with the container of onion butter.

At the table add the onion butter to the noodles. With 2 forks, toss the noodles vigorously; then sprinkle in 1 cup of the grated Parmesan cheese. Continue lifting and mixing the noodles until they're well coated with the cheese. Season with salt and pepper and grate nutmeg over noodles (or use about ⅛ teaspoon ground nutmeg). Pass additional grated Parmesan to sprinkle over individual portions. Makes 4 servings.

Browned Italian Sausages

In a wide frying pan, place 1½ pounds mild Italian pork sausage and add water to cover. Over high heat bring water to boiling; then simmer gently, uncovered, for 20 minutes. Drain well. (If done ahead, cool; then wrap and refrigerate.)

To serve, cut sausages into large chunks and place them in a frying pan over medium heat; cook, turning as needed, until well browned on all sides. Makes 4 servings.

Picnic Time

Take-out Chicken
German-Style Potato Salad
Buttered Rolls or
Thin-Sliced Pumpernickel Bread
Basket of Strawberries
Assorted Cookies

Everything about this menu allows you to just pick up and go once you have the potato salad made. With all the convenient take-out chicken stores around, you can stop by one on your way to the park or out of town.

The salad combines potatoes with bacon and onion; then a creamy, slightly sweet, cooked dressing is added.

German-Style Potato Salad

Cook 2 pounds (6 medium-sized) white new potatoes in boiling water until just tender when pierced (about 30 minutes); drain. When potatoes are cool enough to handle, peel and cut into ½-inch cubes. Thinly slice 1 small, mild, red onion; separate into rings and add to potatoes. Cook 10 slices of bacon until crisp; drain and crumble 7 slices into the potatoes. Set the remaining bacon aside for garnish.

In a saucepan, slightly beat 1 egg; stir in ½ cup sugar, 1 tablespoon all-purpose flour, ½ teaspoon each dry mustard and salt, and ⅓ cup each water and white wine vinegar. Cook over medium heat, stirring, until mixture thickens (about 4 minutes). Pour over potatoes; mix well and season to taste with salt and pepper. Cool, cover, and chill at least 4 hours or overnight. Before serving, garnish the potato salad with the reserved bacon slices, crumbled. Makes 6 to 8 servings.

Summer Salmon Supper

The salmon hides under a deliciously seasoned sour cream mask and cooks in less than thirty minutes. It can be made early in the morning and refrigerated.

The Sesame Cauliflower Sauté goes together rapidly. A generous amount of parsley and green onion gives color and freshness to the dish.

Limestone Salad with Shallot Dressing

Line 6 individual salad plates with 3 or 4 red leaf or butter lettuce leaves. Arrange equally on the lettuce about ½ pound limestone lettuce, separated into individual leaves. Blend together 2 tablespoons wine vinegar, 1 teaspoon Dijon mustard, 2 tablespoons minced shallots (fresh or freeze-dried), ¼ teaspoon salt, and 7 tablespoons olive oil or salad oil. Spoon dressing equally over each salad and serve at once. Makes 6 servings.

Salmon with Sour Cream Mask

4 salmon steaks
1 tablespoon grated onion
   Juice of ½ lemon
½ teaspoon salt
¼ teaspoon pepper
⅛ teaspoon each paprika and liquid
   hot pepper seasoning
½ cup sour cream

Place salmon in a greased, shallow baking dish. Combine onion, lemon juice, salt, pepper, paprika, and liquid hot pepper seasoning. Spread over salmon. Spread sour cream on top of onion seasoning to cover surface of fish. Cover and refrigerate at this point, if you wish.

Bake in a 350° oven for 20 minutes (30 minutes if refrigerated) or until fish flakes when tested with a fork. Makes 4 servings.

Sesame Cauliflower Sauté

1 head cauliflower (about 2 lbs.)
¼ cup sesame seed
4 tablespoons butter or margarine
1 small onion, chopped
¼ cup water
½ cup sliced green onions
¼ cup chopped parsley
   Salt and pepper
   Lemon wedges

Discard leaves from cauliflower and break into flowerets. Cut each floweret through the stem into ¼-inch slices; set aside.

Place the sesame seed in a large frying pan over medium heat; cook, shaking the pan frequently, until seed is golden; set aside. To the pan, add the butter and onion and cook until onion is limp. Add the cauliflower and water; cover and cook until just tender when pierced (about 10 minutes); stir often. Stir in the green onions, parsley, sesame seed, and salt and pepper to taste. Cook, stirring, for 1 to 2 minutes. Turn into a serving dish and pass lemon wedges to squeeze over. Makes 3 to 4 large servings.

Chilled Olallieberry Soup

    1 cup water
      Sugar to taste (or about ⅔ cup)
    4 cups fresh olallieberries (or any tart
      berry—boysenberry, raspberry, or
      loganberry)
    1½ tablespoons cornstarch
    2 tablespoons water
      About 1 cup whipping cream
      (optional)

In a saucepan, bring to a boil the 1 cup water and sugar. Add olallieberries; bring to a boil again. Cook 1 or 2 minutes, taking care that the berries do not overcook and fall apart. Blend cornstarch with 2 tablespoons water. Stir into berry mixture. Stirring gently, bring to a boil again. Allow to cool; chill. Serve in sherbet glasses. Pass cream to pour over top, if desired. Makes 4 servings.

Chile Ahead of Time

Corn Chip Chile
Iceberg Lettuce Wedges and Dressing
Corn Chips
Pineapple Bars
Iced Tea

From a few cans in your cupboard come the ingredients for this speedy chile. You assemble it ahead, ready to heat in the oven a short time before serving. Serve additional corn chips alongside.

Crisp iceberg lettuce wedges make a cool contrast topped with your favorite dressing.

Make the Pineapple Bars ahead, giving them time to cool.

Corn Chip Chile

    3 cans (15 oz. each) red kidney beans,
      drained
    2 cans (about 10 oz. each) enchilada
      sauce
    2 cups shredded Cheddar cheese
    1½ tablespoons chile powder
    1 package (5 oz.) corn chips
    1½ pounds lean ground beef
    1½ cups chopped onions
    1 clove garlic, minced
    2 tablespoons salad oil or olive oil
      Sour cream

Combine the kidney beans, enchilada sauce, Cheddar cheese, chile powder, and corn chips. In a frying pan over medium-high heat, sauté ground beef, onions, and garlic in oil until meat is brown and onions are tender. Discard any fat. Stir together meat and bean mixture; pour into a 3-quart baking dish, and bake, uncovered, in a 350° oven for about 30 minutes until hot and bubbly. Remove from oven, top with dollops of sour cream. Return to oven and heat for 5 minutes longer. Makes 8 to 10 servings.

Pineapple Bars

    1 cup all-purpose flour
    1 teaspoon baking powder
    ½ cup (¼ lb.) butter or margarine
    2 eggs
    1 tablespoon milk
    1 can (about 1 lb. 4 oz.) crushed
      pineapple, drained
    ¼ cup melted butter
    1 cup sugar
    1 cup flaked coconut
    1 teaspoon vanilla

Sift flour before measuring, then sift again with the baking powder. With pastry blender, cut in the ½ cup butter or margarine until mixture is crumbly. Beat 1 egg with the milk; stir into flour mixture. Spread over bottom of 8-inch-square baking pan. Spread pineapple over top. Beat remaining 1 egg thoroughly; stir in melted butter, sugar, flaked coconut, and vanilla. Spread this topping over pineapple. Bake in a 350° oven for 35 to 40 minutes. Cool and cut into about 16 squares.

Cook's Discovery

Poached Turbot with Guacamole
Warm Corn Tortillas
Spanish Rice
Graham Cracker Brownies

Greenland turbot deserves to be discovered for its own unique qualities. It compares to salmon in richness, having tender but firm flesh; its flavor is sweet and mild—reminding some people of crabmeat. It can be cooked and served hot in this recipe or chilled and served deliciously cold.

Wrap the corn tortillas in foil and place in a warm oven just until heated through. Use a packaged Spanish rice mix for quicker serving. The brownies can be made whenever you have time.

Poached Turbot with Guacamole

    2 cups water
    1 small onion, sliced
    3 whole black peppers
    1 whole allspice
    2 tablespoons lime juice or lemon
         juice
    1 teaspoon salt
       1½ to 2 pounds Greenland turbot
         fillets, thawed if frozen
       Guacamole Sauce (recipe follows)
       Lime slices for garnish (optional)

In a wide frying pan, combine the water, onion, pepper, allspice, lime juice, and salt. Bring to boiling and simmer for about 10 minutes. Cut fish into serving-sized pieces and set into pan. Cover and simmer gently until fish flakes when tested with a fork (about 6 minutes). With a wide spatula, carefully remove fish from liquid and arrange on serving plate.

Serve hot with the Guacamole Sauce. Or cover the plate and chill fish and the guacamole separately. Garnish the hot fish with thin slices of lime. Spread guacamole over top of chilled fish. Makes 6 servings.

Guacamole Sauce. Combine 1 can (about 8 oz.) thawed frozen avocado dip with ¼ cup sour cream, 2 green onions (thinly sliced), 1 tablespoon finely chopped parsley, 1 tablespoon lime or lemon juice, ½ teaspoon salt, ⅛ teaspoon liquid hot pepper seasoning, and ½ teaspoon ground coriander (optional). Stir until blended.

Graham Cracker Brownies

    2 eggs
    ½ cup sugar
    ½ cup firmly packed brown sugar
       Dash salt
   14 square graham crackers, crushed fine
         (about 1 cup plus 2 tablespoons)
    ½ cup chopped nuts
    ½ teaspoon vanilla

Beat eggs until light. Mix sugar, salt, graham cracker crumbs, and nuts; add to beaten egg, mixing well; add vanilla.

Spread mixture evenly in a greased, flour-dusted 8-inch-square pan and bake in a 350° oven for 25 to 30 minutes. While brownies are still warm, cut into strips about 1 inch wide and 2 inches long. Makes 2½ dozen cookies.

Buffet Casserole Supper

Beef and Mushroom Bake

Sliced Tomatoes with Oil and Vinegar Dressing

Hot French Rolls

Scarlet Fruit Melange

The main dish is a flavorful baked version of the famous Joe's Special with a bubbly cheese topping. You can assemble it ahead and bake just before serving.

Make and chill the fruit melange for about 2 hours, giving the juices and flavors time to interweave. The syrup turns ruby and the fruits take on a citrus tang.

Beef and Mushroom Bake

- 2 packages (10 or 12 oz. each) frozen chopped spinach
- 1 teaspoon salt
- 1 pound lean ground beef
- 1 large onion, finely chopped
- ½ pound mushrooms, sliced
- 1 cup sour cream
- 1½ teaspoons Italian herb seasoning (or ½ teaspoon each oregano, basil, and thyme leaves)
- ⅛ teaspoon ground nutmeg
- 1 cup each shredded Cheddar and grated Parmesan cheese

Place spinach in a wire strainer; rinse with hot water until thawed; then press out all the water. Set it aside. Sprinkle salt in a large frying pan; place over medium-high heat and crumble in the ground beef; sauté 2 to 3 minutes, add onion and mushrooms, and cook until most of the liquid is gone (about 5 minutes longer). Remove from heat and stir in the spinach, sour cream, Italian seasoning, nutmeg, and ½ cup each of Cheddar and Parmesan cheese. Turn into a shallow, 2-quart casserole; sprinkle remaining cheese over top.

Bake, uncovered, in a 350° oven until heated through (about 20 minutes). Makes 4 to 6 servings.

Scarlet Fruit Melange

Grated peel and juice of 1 each orange, lemon, and lime
- 1 cup sugar
- 3 cups watermelon chunks
- 2 cups strawberries
- 1½ cups raspberries or blueberries (or some of each)
- 5 small peaches, peeled and halved

In a saucepan, place the grated peel and juice of the orange, lemon, and lime. Add sugar, bring to a boil; simmer, stirring, until sugar is dissolved and syrup is slightly thickened. Chill.

In a large bowl, gently mix together the watermelon chunks, strawberries, raspberries or blueberries, and peaches. Pour on the chilled syrup; cover, and chill for 2 hours, carefully stirring once or twice. Serve in dessert bowls. Makes 8 servings.

Dinners for Two

Italian-Style Dinner for Two

Veal Strips with Artichokes

Buttered Green Noodles

Sliced Tomatoes and Avocado

Oil and Vinegar Dressing

Bread Sticks or Crusty Rolls   Butter

Orange Espresso

Veal is a good dinner entrée for two—it's festive yet quick to prepare. For an accompanying salad, peel and slice 2 medium-sized tomatoes; then pit, peel, and slice 1 avocado. Arrange on a platter and pour over about ⅓ cup of your favorite oil and vinegar dressing, coating the avocado well so it won't turn brown. Cover and chill.

You can pound and cut the veal ahead. Then sauté the meat and make the sauce while you cook the noodles.

Veal Strips with Artichokes

¾ pound boneless veal, in ¼-inch-thick slices

2 tablespoons all-purpose flour

¼ teaspoon salt

⅛ teaspoon each pepper and paprika

1 jar (6 oz.) marinated artichoke hearts

1 medium-sized onion, sliced
Butter

¼ cup regular-strength chicken broth

1 tablespoon lemon juice

½ cup sour cream

2 tablespoons grated Parmesan cheese
Hot cooked green noodles

Trim all membrane from veal slices; place each piece between 2 pieces of waxed paper and pound with a mallet until it's about ⅛-inch thick. Cut each piece into ¾-inch-wide strips. Combine the flour, salt, pepper, and paprika. Dredge meat in flour mixture, shaking off excess.

Drain the artichoke liquid into a 10-inch frying pan (reserve artichokes for garnish); cook over medium heat until bubbly. Add meat strips, a few at a time, and sauté until well browned (3 to 5 minutes); lift out and set aside. When all the meat is browned, add onion to pan and butter, if needed; sauté onion 5 minutes. Add broth and stir to loosen browned bits. Stir in lemon juice, sour cream, cheese, and veal strips. Heat through and serve over noodles. Garnish with artichoke hearts. Serves 2.

Orange Espresso

Prepare 3 cups espresso coffee. Pour warm water into 2 glasses (about 8 oz. *each*) to heat them, and then drain. Pour in hot espresso, filling about ⅔ full. Whip ½ cup cream and spoon a heaping tablespoon of it into each glass. Use a vegetable peeler to cut 2 or 3 thin strips of orange peel; then cut into fine slivers. Sprinkle orange peel on cream and garnish with semi-sweet chocolate curls. Makes 2 servings with enough for refills.

Broiled Skewer Dinner

Liver and Bacon with Cabbage

Crusty Dinner Rolls

Casaba Melon with Lime Wedges

While the liver and bacon skewers broil, you can lightly cook the cabbage on top of the range. Together they make a hearty meal. Serve the skewers right on top of the lightly cooked cabbage. Complete the menu with crusty dinner rolls and casaba melon with lime wedges as a meal opener or for dessert.

Liver and Bacon with Cabbage

¾ pound chicken livers
4 tablespoons soy sauce
4 slices bacon
2 tablespoons butter or margarine
4 cups shredded cabbage
1 medium-sized onion, sliced
1 tablespoon dry white wine or Sherry

Cut livers into bite-sized pieces; place in a bowl with 3 tablespoons of the soy; let stand about 15 minutes. Drain. To assemble each skewer, pierce one end of a bacon strip with a small skewer, thread on a piece of liver, then ripple bacon over and under 2 or 3 more pieces of liver to the other end of the bacon slice. Arrange skewers on the rack of a broiler pan and broil, about 4 inches from heat, turning as needed, until bacon is crisp on all sides (about 10 minutes).

Meanwhile, melt the butter in a frying pan; add cabbage and onion, cover, and cook over medium heat, stirring often, until cabbage is just tender to bite (about 8 minutes). Stir in the remaining soy and wine; turn into a serving dish and top with skewers. Serves 2.

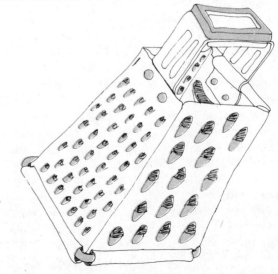

Seafood Ramekins for Two

Butter Lettuce and Cherry Tomatoes
Oil and Vinegar Dressing
Shrimp and Mushroom Ramekins
Buttered Broccoli
One-Egg Pound Cake

Simply cook the broccoli and toss the salad while the ramekins heat. You bake the pound cake in a miniature loaf pan (about 3⅜ by 7⅜ inches or one of similar size that holds 1½ cups) while the shrimp cooks. They both come out of the oven at about the same time. Let the cake cool during dinner.

Shrimp and Mushroom Ramekins

    4   tablespoons butter or margarine
    ¾   pound medium-sized shrimp, shelled
          and deveined
    ¼   pound mushrooms, sliced
    2   tablespoons chopped green onion
    2   tablespoons all-purpose flour
    ⅛   teaspoon Dijon mustard
    ⅓   cup regular-strength chicken broth
    ¼   cup whipping cream
    2   tablespoons dry Sherry
          Salt and pepper
    ½   cup shredded Swiss cheese

Melt 2 tablespoons of the butter in a frying pan over medium heat; add the shrimp and sauté, stirring often until shrimp are pink and tender when pierced (5 to 7 minutes). Transfer shrimp to 2 individual baking dishes or ramekins.

To the pan, add the remaining butter, mushrooms, and green onion. Cook, stirring, until mushrooms are golden brown; sprinkle in flour and cook until bubbly. Gradually stir in the mustard, broth, and cream. Cook, stirring until thickened and bubbly. Stir in Sherry and salt and pepper to taste; spoon evenly over shrimp and sprinkle with cheese. Heat, uncovered, in a 325° oven for 10 to 15 minutes. Serves 2.

One-Egg Pound Cake

    4   tablespoons very soft butter
    ½   cup unsifted powdered sugar
    1   egg, separated
    ¼   teaspoon vanilla
    ⅔   cup sifted cake flour (or sift and
          measure ½ cup regular all-purpose
          flour)
    ¼   cup unsifted powdered sugar
    2   teaspoons milk
    1 or 2 drops of yellow food coloring
          (optional)

With a spoon, stir together the butter and ½ cup powdered sugar. Add the egg yolk to the butter mixture, stirring vigorously until very smoothly blended. Add egg white and vanilla; mix well. Add the flour and stir until batter is smoothly blended.

Spoon batter into a greased, flour-dusted, miniature loaf pan (about 3⅜ by 7⅜ inches) or baking pan that can hold a total of about 1½ cups when full. Bake on lowest rack in a 325° oven for 15 to 25 minutes (depending on pan size) until a wooden pick inserted in center comes out clean and cake is lightly browned. Invert out of pan onto a rack to cool.

For icing, mix together the ¼ cup unsifted powdered sugar and the milk; tint with food coloring, if desired. Drizzle over cake; serve when icing is dry. Makes 2 servings.

Candlelight Dinner

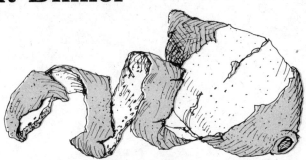

Sole Florentine
Mixed Wild Rice
Buttered Carrots
Three-Ounce Cream Cheese Cake

Rolled sole fillets in creamy sauce bake on top of a bed of spinach for the main dish. Bake them in a 1-quart baking dish or in individual ramekins for easy service.

While the sole bakes, prepare a wild rice mix according to package directions and cook and butter the carrots.

You'll need to bake the cheesecake ahead so it can chill thoroughly before serving. It bakes in a miniature baking pan with a spring release or in any 4½ by 5-inch-diameter round or square pan, making just enough for two.

Sole Florentine

4 small (¾ to 1 lb.) sole fillets
1 bottle (8 oz.) clam juice
1 package (10 oz.) frozen chopped
    spinach, thawed
4 tablespoons grated Parmesan cheese
2 tablespoons each butter or
    margarine and all-purpose flour
⅔ cup milk
⅛ teaspoon ground nutmeg
¼ teaspoon dry mustard
1 tablespoon each lemon juice and
    instant minced onion
    Chopped parsley

Loosely roll each fillet and secure with a pick. In a pan bring clam juice to boiling; set in sole, cover, and simmer for 2 to 3 minutes or until opaque white. Remove fish and drain. Boil clam juice until reduced to ½ cup; pour into cup.

Meanwhile, drain spinach well; distribute over bottom of a shallow 1-quart baking dish or individual ramekins. Sprinkle with 1 tablespoon of the Parmesan. Remove picks and arrange fish on spinach. Melt butter in the pan, blend in flour,

and cook, stirring until bubbly. Remove from heat and gradually stir in milk and clam juice; cook and stir until thickened. Add nutmeg, mustard, lemon juice, and onion. Spoon sauce over fish and spinach. Sprinkle with remaining 3 tablespoons cheese.

Bake, uncovered, in a 425° oven for 10 to 15 minutes or until bubbly and lightly browned. Garnish with chopped parsley. Makes 2 servings.

Three-Ounce Cream Cheese Cake

3 tablespoons all-purpose flour
1 tablespoon sugar
1 tablespoon butter or margarine
1 small (3 oz.) package cream cheese
    (at room temperature)
1 tablespoon sugar
⅛ teaspoon grated lemon peel
¼ teaspoon vanilla
1 egg
2 tablespoons sour cream
1 teaspoon sugar

In a small bowl combine the flour, 1 tablespoon sugar, and butter; rub with your fingers until evenly mixed. Pour into a 4½ to 5-inch-diameter round or square pan (or one of equivalent size) and press firmly in bottom. Bake in a 325° oven for 15 to 20 minutes or until crust is lightly browned. Remove from oven.

Meanwhile, mash cream cheese with a fork, blending with the other 1 tablespoon sugar and the lemon peel. Add vanilla and egg; mash and beat to mix as well as possible. Pour into the baked crust. Bake cake in a 325° oven for 15 minutes or until it appears set when pan is gently jiggled.

Mix the sour cream with the 1 teaspoon sugar. When you take the cheesecake from the oven, spread with sour cream at once. Chill, then serve. Makes 2 servings.

Broiler Dinner

Your broiler does most of the work for this easily prepared supper. Heat 1 package (12 oz.) frozen potato puffs under the broiler along with the pork chops and tomatoes.

Top off the dinner with broiled pears filled with currant jelly.

Lemon-Glazed Pork Chops

Preheat the broiler. Allow 1 or 2 shoulder pork chops (each cut about ¾ inch thick) for each serving. Broil chops 3 or 4 inches from heat until well browned; season with salt and pepper; turn and broil other side. Spoon Lemon Glaze (recipe follows) over each chop. Top with thin lemon slices and return to broiler until glaze bubbles and browns slightly. Serves 2.

Lemon Glaze. Blend 2 to 3 teaspoons prepared mustard, ½ teaspoon grated lemon peel, and 1 tablespoon lemon juice with ½ cup firmly packed brown sugar.

Basil-Topped Tomatoes

Cut one large tomato in thick slices. Brush slices with melted butter. Then season with salt and a sprinkle of basil leaves. Slip under the broiler briefly, just until hot. Serves 2.

Broiled Pears with Currant Jelly

Cut 2 firm-ripe pears in half, peel, and core; brush each half with melted butter. Place pear halves, cut side down on a broiler rack and broil 5 minutes. Turn pears over, dot with butter, and continue broiling for 5 minutes. Fill the hollow of each pear half with a dollop of currant jelly. Serve hot. Makes 2 servings.

Intimate Dinner for Two

Have a feast on cold-cooked shrimp in the shell, artichoke, and cucumber slices with a homemade Lemon-Dill Mayonnaise for dipping all three. Precede the cold fingerfood platter with a hot soup. You might try mixing a can (10 oz.) cream of asparagus soup with 1 can milk; heat, stirring until hot. Then add 2 tablespoons dry vermouth.

Accompany the soup and shrimp platter with thick slices of crusty bread and a pot of butter. You might also wish to include finger bowls on your table.

For dessert, offer sweet crackers and breakfast cheese.

Shrimp-Artichoke Platter with Lemon-Dill Mayonnaise

¾ pound medium-sized raw shrimp in
    shells
1 quart boiling salted water
2½ quarts water
4 tablespoons vinegar
2 tablespoons salad oil
1 teaspoon salt
1 large artichoke
    Lemon-Dill Mayonnaise (recipe
     follows)
1 small cucumber
    Sprigs of watercress (optional)
    Lemon wedges (optional)

To devein shrimp, insert a sharp skewer beneath the vein in about the middle of the back and carefully pull the vein out. If the vein breaks, insert the pick in another place and repeat.

Add shrimp to the 1 quart boiling salted water and simmer, uncovered, about 5 minutes or until shrimp are pink and firm. Drain, cover, and chill until ready to serve.

Bring to boiling the 2½ quarts water with the vinegar, salad oil, and salt. Slice about ½ inch off the top of the artichoke; break off small leaves at base and cut thorny tips from exterior leaves with scissors; place the artichoke in boiling water. Cover and simmer until stem end pierces readily (about 40 to 50 minutes). Lift from cooking liquid and drain; cut base flat, cover, and chill until serving time.

To serve, slightly open center leaves of cold artichoke with fingertips; pluck out the thin inner leaves and with a small spoon scoop out the fuzzy choke. Fill hollow with Lemon-Dill Mayonnaise (recipe follows). Place in the center of a large platter and surround with shrimp and cucumber slices. If desired, garnish with sprigs of watercress and lemon wedges. Makes 2 servings.

Lemon-Dill Mayonnaise. Combine in a blender jar 1 egg yolk, 1 tablespoon lemon juice, 1½ teaspoons white wine vinegar, ½ teaspoon each sugar and dry mustard, and ¼ teaspoon salt; whirl just until blended. With blender turned on, gradually pour in ½ cup salad oil; blend smooth. Stir in ¼ teaspoon dill weed; cover and chill.

Roast Pork Tenderloin Dinner

**Pork Tenderloin with Onion-Apple
Cream**

Wheat Pilaf

Green Beans

Romaine Cucumber Salad

**Orange Segments with Orange-Flavored
Liqueur**

Baste a small whole pork tenderloin with Sherry-flavored cream as it roasts. The same basting sauce flavors slow-cooked onions and apples.

While the pork is in the oven, you have time to prepare the pilaf. Also mix torn romaine leaves with sprigs of watercress, cucumber slices, and

Italian dressing for the salad. Then about 5 minutes before the pork is done, cook about ½ pound green beans (strings and ends removed) in boiling salted water to cover until barely tender (about 5 minutes); drain.

For a refreshing dessert, marinate orange segments in a little orange-flavored liqueur.

(Continued on next page)

Pork Tenderloin with Onion-Apple Cream

1 whole pork tenderloin (about 12 oz.)
6 tablespoons whipping cream
2 tablespoons cream Sherry
1 teaspoon Dijon mustard
½ teaspoon each salt and horseradish
2 tablespoons butter
1 large onion, thinly sliced
1 small Golden Delicious apple, thinly
    sliced
    Parsley sprigs

Place the pork on a rack set in a baking pan; insert a meat thermometer into the thickest part and place in a 425° oven.

Stir together the whipping cream, Sherry, mustard, salt, and horseradish. Brush mixture over pork frequently during roasting; roast 25 to 30 minutes or until thermometer registers 170°.

Melt the butter in a wide frying pan over medium heat and cook the onion and apple, stirring frequently, until limp and golden (about 20 minutes). Add remaining cream baste to onion and apple mixture and bring to a boil; place in a small bowl and keep warm. Arrange pork on a small board or platter and garnish with parsley sprigs. Serve with onion-apple cream to spoon over. Makes 2 servings.

Wheat Pilaf

1 tablespoon butter or margarine
1 tablespoon minced onion
½ cup bulgur or quick-cooking cracked
    wheat
1 cup regular-strength beef broth
2 tablespoons minced parsley
    Salt to taste

Melt the butter in a pan over medium heat, add onion and bulgur, and cook until onion is tender. Stir in the beef broth and parsley; cover and simmer about 15 minutes or until liquid is absorbed. Add salt to taste, dot with additional butter, if desired, and serve. Makes 2 servings.

Lamb for Two

Rack of Lamb with Parsley Butter

Small New Potatoes

Fresh Broccoli

Butter Lettuce with Oil and Vinegar Dressing

Vanilla Ice Cream with Crème de Menthe

Elegant rack of lamb is featured in this dinner for two. The rack, consisting of about 8 small chops, is perfectly sized for 2 servings (the meat portion in each chop is small). Here the lamb is rubbed with a parsley-flavored butter, which also goes over the baked potatoes and broccoli.

For the salad, simply mix torn butter lettuce with oil and vinegar dressing. A scoop of vanilla ice cream with a little crème de menthe poured over makes a quick dessert.

Rack of Lamb Dinner with Parsley Butter

Purchase a Frenched rack of lamb (meat removed from ends of chop bones) with about 8 ribs. Rub about 1½ tablespoons of the Parsley Butter (recipe follows) over lamb and place in a shallow roasting pan with rib bones pointing downward. Insert meat thermometer in thickest part of roast without touching bone. Lay 4 or 5 small new potatoes (about 2½ inches in diameter) in pan beside meat.

Place in a 425° oven and cook about 35 minutes or until meat thermometer reads 145° for medium-rare. Potatoes are done when they give readily to pressure (takes 35 to 40 minutes). If meat is done before potatoes, remove meat from pan and keep warm while the potatoes bake.

About 5 minutes before potatoes are done, cook ¾ pound broccoli in boiling salted water to cover until barely tender (about 5 minutes). Arrange lamb and potatoes (cut gash in top, press sides to force open) on a platter; serve the broccoli alongside.

To serve, cut lamb between ribs. Offer Parsley Butter to spoon over vegetables and lamb. Makes 2 servings.

Parsley Butter

    6 tablespoons soft butter or margarine
    ⅓ cup minced parsley
    1 clove garlic, minced or mashed
    ½ teaspoon salt
    ¼ teaspoon pepper

Mix together in a small bowl the butter, parsley, garlic, salt, and pepper until well blended. Rub into lamb; serve on baked potatoes and broccoli.

Beef and Tomatoes in a Wok

Beef with Tomatoes
Crispy Translucent Noodles
Fresh Pineapple Slices

Cooking with a wok is speedy and rewarding. If you cook with electricity, preheat the element for several minutes; then cook as with gas, placing the wok directly on the preheated element. You can fry the crispy noodles up to a day ahead. Have all the ingredients cut and measured and the cooking sauce prepared before you start to cook.

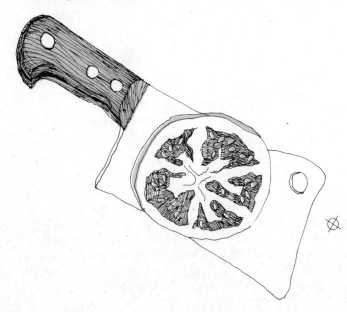

Beef with Tomatoes

    1 pound boneless, lean beef thinly
        sliced across grain into pieces
        about ⅛ inch thick and 1 inch
        square
    2 tablespoons soy sauce
    1 teaspoon each sugar and minced or
        grated fresh ginger
    1 clove garlic, minced
        About 5 tablespoons salad oil
    1 medium-sized onion, cut in 1-inch
        squares (separate layers)
    ¼ pound mushrooms, sliced through
        stems
    1 medium-sized green pepper, cut in
        1-inch squares
    1 basket (about 14 oz.) cherry
        tomatoes, halved
        Cooking Sauce (directions follow)
        Crispy Translucent Noodles,
        optional (directions follow)
        Shredded lettuce

Combine the beef with the soy sauce, sugar, minced ginger, and garlic. Place wok over high heat. Put 1 tablespoon oil into the wok and, when hot, add half of the meat mixture; stir and fry until browned (about 2 minutes). Turn out of pan. Repeat, using 1 more tablespoon oil and remaining meat.

Reheat wok, add 3 tablespoons oil, and when hot, add onion and mushrooms; stir and fry for 2 minutes. Add green pepper; stir and fry for 30 seconds. Return meat to pan, add tomatoes, and stir-fry a few seconds. Add Cooking Sauce; cook and stir until it boils and thickens (about 3 minutes). Pour into serving dish or over the crispy noodles. Makes 2 to 4 servings.

Cooking Sauce. Combine 1 tablespoon each cornstarch and sugar with ½ teaspoon salt; blend in 2 tablespoons soy sauce and ½ cup regular-strength beef broth.

Crispy Translucent Noodles. You'll need 2 to 3 ounces of the special translucent noodles (look for them in Oriental markets); they may be called rice sticks, yam noodles, or bean threads.

To cook the noodles, pour salad oil into the wok to about 1 inch deep (steady the wok in a ring stand); heat oil to about 400°. Drop in a small handful of the noodles at a time. As they puff up, push them down into the oil; then turn the entire mass over. When the noodles are lightly browned and stop crackling (about 1½ minutes), remove and drain. Skim oil before frying the next handful. (If done ahead, cool and package airtight in plastic bags.) To serve, line a platter with shredded lettuce, arranging noodles on top; then spoon over the Beef with Tomatoes.

Skillet Sausage Sauté

Polish Sausage and Potatoes
Apple Rings
Sliced Tomato Cucumber Salad
Raspberry Yogurt Parfait

You use the same frying pan to cook each of the elements for this hearty entrée. Start by browning the sausage. While it cooks, prepare the vegetables and apple. Serve the sausage with mustard and horseradish. Accompany with a plate of sliced tomatoes and cucumbers, topped with your favorite salad dressing.

Serve Raspberry Yogurt Parfaits in tall, slender wine glasses if you don't have parfait glasses.

Polish Sausage and Potatoes

About 6 tablespoons butter
About 12 ounces kielbasa sausage
2 medium-sized potatoes, peeled and
    thinly sliced
1 large onion, thinly sliced
1 large Golden Delicious apple

Melt 1 tablespoon of the butter in a frying pan over medium heat. Slash sausage at 1-inch inter-

vals and cook until browned on all sides. Arrange on a warm serving dish; keep warm.

Add 4 tablespoons of the butter to the pan; add the potatoes and onion and stir well. Cover and cook, stirring often and adding more butter, if needed, until potatoes are tender (about 15 minutes). Remove the lid and continue cooking until potatoes are browned; arrange with the sausage; keep warm.

Peel and core the apple; cut into ½-inch-thick rings. Melt 1 more tablespoon butter in the pan; add apple and sauté until lightly browned on both sides. Arrange with sausage and potatoes. Makes 2 servings.

Raspberry Yogurt Parfait

1 egg white
¼ cup firmly packed brown sugar
1 cup plain or vanilla-flavored yogurt
1 tablespoon orange-flavored liqueur
    or thawed frozen orange juice concentrate
2 packages (10 oz. each) frozen
    raspberries, thawed and drained

Beat the egg white until stiff; then gradually add the brown sugar, beating until glossy. Fold in the yogurt and orange-flavored liqueur or orange juice concentrate. Alternate raspberries with yogurt sauce in parfait glasses or in 6-ounce tall, slender wine glasses. Fills 4 glasses.

Dinner on a Steak Plate

Blue Cheese Dip   Vegetable Relishes
Broiled Skirt Steaks
Hot Asparagus Spears
Cherry Tomatoes in Butter
No-Bake Choco-Nut Cookies

Serve the whole dinner on a steak platter for convenience. Just broil the skirt steaks and transfer to heated steak plates. Sauté halved cherry tomatoes in a little butter to accompany the steak. The zestful cheese sauce enhances both the salad-dipping vegetables and the skirt steaks, making enough for two entrées.

The cookies are a busy cook's dream. You just whip all the ingredients together and drop them onto waxed paper to let them firm up a few minutes.

Plan to mix and chill the cheese dip first. Cut up the vegetables and refrigerate them. While the skirt steaks broil, cook the asparagus spears and cherry tomatoes.

Blue Cheese Dip

    1 small package (3 oz.) cream cheese
    2 ounces (¼ cup) blue cheese
    1 tablespoon each finely chopped
         green onion and parsley
    ½ teaspoon each Worcestershire and
         horseradish
    ½ teaspoon garlic salt
    ⅓ cup unflavored yogurt
       4 or 5 mushrooms, sliced
    1 zucchini, sliced
    1 carrot, sliced

Beat together the cream cheese, blue cheese, green onion, parsley, Worcestershire, horseradish, garlic salt, and yogurt. Spoon into a bowl, cover, and chill.

Serve half the sauce with the mushrooms, zucchini, and carrot; the other half with the skirt steaks. Makes about 1 cup sauce.

Broiled Skirt Steaks

Buy 2 skirt steaks, untenderized, wrapped in a pinwheel and skewered (about 6 ounces *each*). Place on a rack in a broiler pan and broil about 4 inches from the heat in a preheated broiler, turning once and allowing about 5 to 7 minutes to a side for rare meat. Season with salt and pepper. Serves 2.

Cherry Tomatoes in Butter

Cut in half 1½ cups cherry tomatoes and heat quickly, uncovered, in 2 teaspoons butter, shaking pan, until hot through. Season with salt and pepper. Makes 2 servings.

No-Bake Choco-Nut Cookies

    3 cups quick-cooking rolled oats
    5 tablespoons cocoa
    ½ cup chopped nuts
    ½ cup shredded coconut
    2 cups sugar
    ½ cup milk
    ½ cup (¼ lb.) butter or margarine

In a bowl combine the oats, cocoa, nuts, and coconut. Place sugar, milk, and butter or margarine in a saucepan and bring just to a boil, stirring to combine; pour over the rolled oats mixture. Mix lightly until blended. Drop teaspoonfuls of batter onto waxed paper or foil. Let stand until firm (about 10 minutes). Makes about 4 dozen cookies.

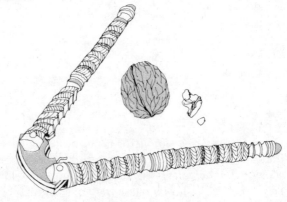

Chicken Sandwich Supper

Chicken Supper Sandwiches
Assorted Relishes and Raw Vegetables
Butter Cookies

You'll need a knife and fork to eat these hearty open-faced chicken breast sandwiches. Accompany them with an assortment of relishes and crisp raw vegetables, such as pickles, ripe olives, carrot and celery sticks, and red or green pepper strips. Serve Butter Cookies for dessert.

Chicken Supper Sandwiches

1 pound chicken breasts
  Salted water
4 slices bacon
2 English muffins, split, toasted, and
  buttered
4 slices mild onion
1 large tomato, peeled and cut into 4
  thick slices
½ cup shredded Longhorn Cheddar
  cheese

Simmer chicken in a small amount of salted water until meat is no longer pink throughout (about 15 minutes); discard skin and bones and slice meat.

Meanwhile, cut bacon slices in half crosswise and partially fry the bacon to remove most of the fat; bacon should still be limp. Set aside. Distribute the chicken evenly over the 4 toasted muffin halves; top each with 1 onion slice and 1 tomato slice. Distribute cheese evenly over each and top each with 2 pieces of bacon. Broil about 4 inches from heat until cheese is bubbly and bacon is crisp (3 to 5 minutes). Makes 2 servings.

Market to Bike-Stop Picnics

Papaya Turkey Salad
Avocado Seafood Salad
Trailside Smørrebrød
Supermarket Antipasto

Bicycling enthusiasts off for a day's outing agree that the exercise and fresh air build hearty appetites. Yet when carrying space is limited, what kind of creative lunch can a bicyclist take along?

All you'll need for these portable meals is a multi-purpose can and bottle opener or folding knife and small metal or plastic eating utensils. In hot weather you may also want a small insulated bag to keep food cool.

Here are four bike-stop picnics that should appeal to many tastes.

Papaya Turkey Salad

For two servings, you'll need 1 large papaya (or cantaloupe), 1 can (5 oz.) boned turkey or chicken, 1 carton (8 oz.) peach or apricot-flavored yogurt, and 1 lime. Cut the papaya in half, scoop out the seeds, and fill the center of each half with boned turkey. Squeeze lime and spoon yogurt over top.

Avocado Seafood Salad

For 2 servings, you'll need 1 large avocado, 1 package (3 oz.) smoked salmon or 1 can (6½ oz.) chunk-style tuna, 1 carton (8 oz.) unflavored yogurt, and 1 lemon. Halve avocado and remove seed; drain tuna, if used. Pile salmon or tuna into each avocado half; squeeze lemon and spoon yogurt over top as you eat.

Trailside Smørrebrød

For two people you'll need 2 or 3 medium-sized cucumbers or zucchini, 1 can (3¼ oz.) kippered herring, 1 carton (8 oz.) refrigerated onion dip, 1 small can (about 8 oz.) pickled beets, and about 1 dozen cherry tomatoes (optional). Cut cucumbers or zucchini across into thick slices as needed; top each slice with some kippered herring and spoon the onion dip over top. Accompany with beets and cherry tomatoes, if you wish.

Supermarket Antipasto

For two people you'll need 1 can (about 3 oz.) sardines (packed in oil or mustard sauce), 1 small can (8 oz.) Italian zucchini (in tomato sauce), 1 small package Westphalian-style pumpernickel bread, 1 package (3 oz.) cream cheese, 1 or 2 dill pickles, and 1 can (about 3 oz.) whole pitted ripe olives. Assemble open-faced sandwiches of bread, cream cheese, sardines, and a spoonful of the zucchini and sauce. Eat out of hand; pass olives and pickles.

Two for Dinner

Chicken Livers with Grapes
Hot Cooked Rice
Butter Lettuce Salad
Fresh Asparagus
Ice Cream

When there's just the two of you, this menu might be the order of the day. It features sautéed livers and hot grapes in a creamy sauce to spoon over rice. Since the entrée cooks quickly, have all the ingredients ready when you begin.

Toss the Butter Lettuce Salad and serve with a dressing of your choice. Quickly steam or boil whole asparagus spears and serve.

Chicken Livers with Grapes

¾ pound chicken livers
  All purpose flour
2 tablespoons butter or margarine
1 tablespoon minced onion
  Dash each ground ginger and pepper
½ teaspoon Worcestershire
¾ cup seedless grapes
3 tablespoons each Sherry and
    regular-strength chicken broth
2 tablespoons sour cream
1 tablespoon chopped parsley

Rinse chicken livers and pat dry with paper towels. Dust lightly with flour. Heat butter over medium-high heat in a frying pan. Add onion and livers. Cook, turning, until browned (3 to 4 minutes). Add salt, ginger, pepper, Worcestershire, grapes, Sherry, and chicken broth. Reduce heat, cover, and cook 3 minutes. Remove from heat; stir in sour cream; heat, stirring, but do not boil. Serve sprinkled with parsley. Makes 2 servings.

Barbecue Dinners

Lamb Kebab Sandwich Picnic

Ground Lamb Kebabs
Arab Bread   Green Pepper Strips
Tomato Wedges   Yogurt Relish
Fresh Fruit

Wrapped in warm Arab bread, ground lamb kebabs make delicious hot sandwiches for a picnic. To make them, press and mold the meat to a skewer, holding it on with a slice of onion and pepper at either end. Heat the bread over the fire in a sturdy frying pan or griddle. Serve with Yogurt Relish and vegetables for a complete meal-in-one. Allow 1 or 2 sandwiches for each serving.

Ground Lamb Kebabs

1 pound ground lamb
2 tablespoons each all-purpose flour and water
1 teaspoon salt
¼ teaspoon each pepper, ground allspice, and ground cinnamon
1 each green pepper and onion, cut in wedges or squares
  Arab bread (also called Armenian or pocket bread, peta, or pita)
  Olive oil
  Yogurt Relish (directions follow)
½ green pepper, thinly sliced
1 tomato, cut in wedges

Mix well with your hands the ground lamb, flour, water, salt, pepper, allspice, and cinnamon. Divide into 4 equal portions and shape like sausages about 5 to 6 inches long. Spear a piece of green pepper on a skewer, then a lamb kebab, pressing and molding the meat to the skewer; enclose meat at other end by a piece of onion. Repeat, putting one or more kebabs on each skewer.

To cook the kebabs, support skewers about 6 inches above a bed of hot glowing coals and turn often until lamb is firm next to skewer (about 12 to 15 minutes).

To heat Arab bread, lightly brush both sides with olive oil. Press one side of the bread, then the other onto a hot skillet or griddle just until they're warm and soft; it takes less than a minute.

Using a folded paper napkin or several thicknesses of paper toweling to protect your hands, grasp a piece of warm Arab bread, fold it around a kebab, and slide it off the skewer along with roasted pepper and onion. To complete each sandwich, tuck in several green pepper strips and tomato wedges and add a spoonful of Yogurt Relish to garnish. Makes 4 sandwiches.

Yogurt Relish. Combine ½ cup unflavored yogurt with ¼ cup chopped onion and 1 teaspoon mild prepared mustard.

Barbecued Bones

Dinosaur Bones
(Marinade variations optional)

Sourdough French Bread

Crunchy Pea Salad

Hot Bananas in the Skin

These are really the ribs that the meatman trims away when he makes a boned and rolled rib roast. A nine-year-old boy named them dinosaur bones because they call for rather primitive eating techniques. The meat that clings to these bones is as tender as the roast, so you can barbecue them a rich brown on the outside, keeping the meat juicy inside.

Occasionally rib bones are on display at meat counters, but since the supply is limited, it's wise to order ahead. (If you have a rib roast boned, be sure to ask for the bones. Freeze the bones until you accumulate enough for a meal; allow about 1 pound or 3 ribs for a serving.)

The ribs are good and flavorful simply barbecued with salt, pepper, and butter as the only seasonings. But they also take well to further embellishments with marinades and bastes. Two different sauces are suggested here.

The ribs cook best over a low, even bed of coals. Make your fire with about 3 dozen briquets. After a good bed of glowing coals forms, spread them evenly under the cooking area of the grill.

Make the salad before your crowd arrives, letting it chill about 30 minutes.

Place bananas on the grill when you take off the bones, turning to cook both sides.

Dinosaur Bones

6 pounds (about 18) meaty beef rib
  bones
Butter or margarine
Salt and pepper

Cut between ribs to separate individual bones. Place meat, bone side up, about 5 inches above glowing coals. Brush with butter occasionally and turn ribs to brown all sides. Cook about 25 minutes for rare meat, 35 minutes for medium-well done. Sprinkle with salt and pepper to taste. Serve directly from barbecue or on a heated platter. Makes about 6 servings.

(Continued on next page)

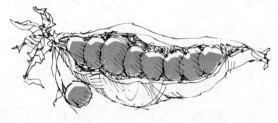

Teriyaki Marinade

For 6 pounds of beef ribs, prepare this marinade: In a small saucepan, combine ¾ cup each water and soy sauce, ⅓ cup sugar, 2 cloves garlic (minced or mashed), 2 teaspoons grated fresh ginger (or 1½ tablespoons chopped preserved ginger), and 2 tablespoons tomato-based chile sauce. Stir over medium heat until sugar dissolves. Let cool.

Separate the rib bones and marinate in the sauce for several hours or overnight. Lift ribs from marinade, gently shaking off excess; barbecue as directed on page 63 for Dinosaur Bones. Baste occasionally with the balance of the marinade instead of using butter.

Tomato-Glazed Marinade

For 6 pounds of beef ribs, prepare this marinade: Heat 2 tablespoons salad oil in a small frying pan over medium-high heat. Add 1 large onion, chopped, and cook, stirring, until golden. Add 1¼ cups catsup, ¼ cup firmly packed brown sugar, 2½ tablespoons Worcestershire, ¾ teaspoon dry mustard, and 2 small, dried hot chile peppers (crumbled, with seeds and pith removed). Bring to boiling; then let cool.

Separate the rib bones and marinate in the sauce for several hours or overnight. Lift ribs from marinade; barbecue as directed on page 63 for Dinosaur Bones. Instead of brushing with butter, use the rest of the marinade.

Crunchy Pea Salad

    1 package (10 oz.) frozen green peas
    1 can (about 6 oz.) water chestnuts,
        drained and sliced
      3 or 4 stalks celery, thinly sliced
    1 cup coarsely shredded carrots
      3 or 4 green onions, thinly sliced
    2 tablespoons each salad oil and wine
        vinegar
    1 tablespoon soy sauce
    1 teaspoon each sugar, paprika, and
        dry mustard
    ½ teaspoon salt
    1 small clove garlic, minced or
        mashed
    4 tablespoons mayonnaise
      Salt and pepper
      Lettuce leaves
      Crisp bacon bits, optional

Pour the peas into a wire strainer and run hot water over them to thaw; drain well. Combine in a bowl the peas, water chestnuts, celery, carrots, and green onions.

Mix together the salad oil, vinegar, soy sauce, sugar, paprika, mustard, the ½ teaspoon salt, and garlic. Beat to blend and pour over pea combination. Mix well and cover. Chill for 30 minutes to an hour.

Shortly before serving, drain off any extra marinade. Mix the mayonnaise into salad; add salt and pepper to taste. Arrange lettuce leaves on salad plates or in a salad bowl. Spoon salad on lettuce. Garnish with crisp bacon bits, if desired. Makes 4 to 6 servings.

Hot Bananas in the Skin

Place 6 whole, unpeeled bananas on the grill about 4 to 6 inches above low-glowing coals. Grill, turning often, until hot throughout and the skin color has turned black (about 8 minutes). Serve with butter and a wedge of lime or lemon. Makes 6 servings.

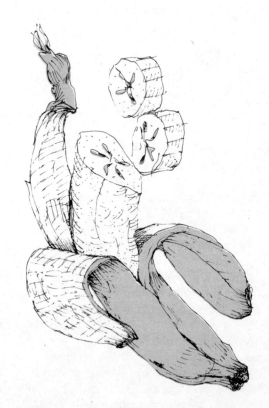

Skewer Supper

Chilled Tangerine Juice
Italian Sausage and Fruit Skewers
Honey Lime Sauce
Hard-Cooked Eggs
Crescent Rolls   Butter

Much of the work for this menu can be done a day ahead, and the serving procedure frees you to join guests. They prepare individual skewers of fruit and precooked sausage, which are basted with a sauce of honey and lime and browned on a small barbecue.

Early in the day, cook the sausages and chill. Also hard-cook the eggs, allowing 1 or 2 for each person. You can do everything else while the barbecue fire is prepared for cooking; reconstitute a 6-ounce can frozen tangerine juice concentrate for each 3 to 4 servings; cut the fruit for the skewers; mix the honey sauce; and heat the rolls (frozen or from a bakery), allowing 1 or 2 for each person.

Italian Sausage and Fruit Skewers

In a wide frying pan, place 2 pounds mild Italian pork sausage and add water to cover. Bring water to boiling over high heat and simmer gently, uncovered, for 20 minutes; drain well. (If done ahead, cool, then wrap and refrigerate.)

Cut the peel from 1 large pineapple; then cut out the core and cut fruit in ¾-inch cubes. Set aside. Scoop out and discard seeds from 1 large cantaloupe; then cut away peel and cut fruit into ¾-inch cubes.

To present, group separately on a large platter the pineapple, cantaloupe, and sausages. Set a knife alongside. Invite guests to prepare their own skewers; they might spear whole sausages and grill them to accompany the cold fruits, or they can combine chunks of sausage and fruit on skewers to brown over the grill. Brush Honey Lime Sauce (recipe follows) on the foods to be grilled, or, if desired, spoon sparingly over the cold fruit.

Place skewers on a hibachi or other small barbecue with grill set 3 to 4 inches above a solid, even layer of fully ignited, glowing coals. Turn skewers until just brown on all sides (about 5 to 7 minutes). Makes 6 to 8 servings.

Honey Lime Sauce. In a small serving dish, stir together ½ cup lime juice and 3 tablespoons honey. Makes about ⅔ cup sauce.

Patio Barbecue Dinner

Barbecued Chicken Bundles
Peanut Potato Salad
Corn-on-the-Cob
Apple Pie á la Mode

There are almost as many versions of barbecued chicken and potato salad as there are cooks. The only constant ingredients in these two favorites are the chicken and the potato.

The succulent chicken bundles are actually two whole chicken legs that you bone and tie together—the boning is easy. And salted peanuts give a unique flavor and crunchiness to the potato salad. Both can be prepared well in advance.

If your barbecue is large enough, cook the corn alongside the chicken. Wrap cleaned and husked individual ears in foil; turn frequently on grill (they take about 25 minutes).

For dessert, you might serve wedges of apple pie (your own or from a bakery) topped with scoops of vanilla ice cream.

(Continued on next page)

Barbecued Chicken Bundles

For each bundle you will need 2 whole chicken legs, drumsticks and thighs attached. To bone each leg, cut all around the bone just above the ankle joint. On the inside of the leg, cut to the bone along the length of the leg. With a knife blade, push and cut meat off the bone. Sprinkle meat with salt, pepper, and minced garlic. If desired, lay a 2-inch sprig of fresh rosemary in the center of one leg.

Place meaty sides together, positioning thigh section of one over drumstick section of the other. Pull loose skin from edges of bottom leg up over top leg, tucking in meat from top leg to make a neat bundle.

Tie with string at about 1½-inch intervals down length of the bundle; then brush it with olive oil. Grill 4 to 6 inches above glowing coals, turning as needed, until well browned on all sides and meat is no longer pink (cut into thickest portion to check), about 40 minutes. Makes 1 large or 2 smaller servings.

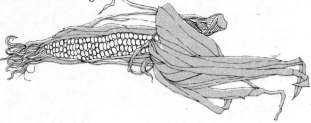

Peanut Potato Salad

        2 pounds red new potatoes
           Boiling salted water
    ½ cup each chopped green pepper and
           celery
    ¾ cup thinly sliced green onion
    ¼ cup each chopped parsley and diced
           cucumber
    ¾ cup salted Spanish peanuts
        6 slices bacon, crisply fried
    ½ cup mayonnaise
        2 tablespoons cider vinegar
        1 tablespoon chunk-style peanut
           butter
        1 teaspoon curry powder (optional)
           Salt and pepper

Cook potatoes in boiling water until just tender when pierced (about 30 minutes). Drain. When cool, peel (if desired) and cut into ½-inch cubes. Combine potatoes with green pepper, celery, green onion, parsley, cucumber, and ½ cup of the nuts. Crumble bacon and mix into salad.

In a small bowl, stir together the mayonnaise, vinegar, peanut butter, and curry powder, if used. Pour over potato mixture and mix well. Season to taste with salt and pepper. Cover and chill at least 4 hours or overnight. Just before serving, stir well and garnish with the remaining salted nuts. Makes about 6 servings.

South-of-the-Border Barbecue

Butter Lettuce and Cherry Tomato
Halves

Oil and Vinegar Dressing

Grilled Ham Steak with
Cantaloupe and Pineapple

Chile and Cheese Rice

Chocolate Coconut
Sundaes

Familiar Mexican flavors spark this colorful, informal dinner for six. The menu centers on a thick ham steak and fresh fruits you glaze over charcoal. Meanwhile, a rice casserole bakes in the oven. You can assemble the rice casserole ahead, ready to put into the oven to heat before serving. It also holds well (with the oven turned off) should dinner be delayed a half hour or so.

For the dessert, toast about ½ cup coconut and prepare your favorite chocolate sauce or purchase one. You'll also need about 1 to 1½-quarts vanilla ice cream.

Use a spicy oil and vinegar dressing (homemade or purchased) to dress the bowl of lettuce and tomatoes.

Grilled Ham Steak with Cantaloupe and Pineapple

For the basting sauce, combine in a small saucepan 2 tablespoons melted butter or margarine, 3 tablespoons honey, ¼ cup lime juice, and a dash of ground nutmeg. Heat, stirring until blended. Set aside; reheat before using.

Slash the outer layer of fat (at about 2-inch intervals) on a center slice of fully cooked ham 1 to 1½ inches thick (about 2½ lbs.). Cut 1 cantaloupe into 6 wedges; remove seeds and peel. Also cut 6 slices (about ¾ inch thick) from 1 ripe pineapple; peel, but leave core in place for easier handling.

To cook, brush both sides of ham steak with basting sauce. Place steak on a grill about 6 inches above medium-hot coals. Cook for 16 to 20 minutes, turning occasionally and basting frequently with the basting sauce. About 8 to 10 minutes before ham is done, brush melon and pineapple with basting sauce; place on grill. Cook fruit, turning and basting often, until glazed and lightly browned on all sides (about 10 minutes).

To serve, arrange ham and fruits on carving board. Cut thin slices across the grain of meat. Serves 6.

Chile and Cheese Rice

> 1 cup long grain rice
>   Boiling salted water
> 1 can (4 oz.) whole California green
>   chiles (seeded and diced)
> 1⅓ cups sour cream
> ½ pound jack cheese, shredded (about
>   2 cups)

Cook rice in boiling water according to package directions. Combine the cooked rice, chiles, sour cream, and 1½ cups of the cheese. Turn into a greased 1½-quart casserole; sprinkle remaining cheese on top. Bake, uncovered, in a 350° oven for about 30 minutes or until cheese is bubbly and rice is heated through. Makes 6 servings.

Mexican Patio Barbecue

Guacamole and Corn Chips
Fresh Orange and Onion Salad
Grilled Steak Cubes and Sausages
Refried Beans   Warm Flour Tortillas
Raspberry Sherbet

When planning a summer barbecue, it never hurts to allow for unexpected guests. This menu can easily be expanded to serve an extra three or four.

To be prepared for additional guests, purchase 2 cans (about 8 oz. each) frozen avocado dip. Also buy 2 cans (about 1 lb. each) refried beans and about 1½ pounds assorted fully-cooked sausages (such as frankfurters, garlic frankfurters, or Polish sausage). Then, if extra guests arrive, you can heat the second can of beans and grill the sausages along with the steak. (Otherwise, the sausages can be the start of another meal.) Thaw the extra can of avocado dip to blend with homemade guacamole or with the other can of avocado dip.

Fresh Orange and Onion Salad

> 4 large oranges
> 1 large mild red onion, thinly sliced
>   crosswise and separated into rings
> ½ cup salad oil
> ¼ cup white wine vinegar
> 2 tablespoons sugar
> ¾ teaspoon paprika
> ½ teaspoon each salt and dry mustard
>   Lettuce leaves

Several hours before serving, cut the peel and white membrane from oranges and slice thinly crosswise; place in a shallow bowl. Tuck onion rings in among orange slices. Blend together the salad oil, vinegar, sugar, paprika, salt, and mustard. Pour dressing over orange and onion slices; cover and refrigerate at least 2 hours.

To serve, lift orange and onion slices from dressing and arrange on lettuce-lined salad plates; serve remaining dressing in a separate container. Makes 6 to 8 servings.

Grilled Steak Cubes and Sausages

In a shallow baking dish, stir together ½ cup olive oil or salad oil; ¼ cup white wine vinegar; 2 tablespoons instant minced onion; ½ teaspoon each salt, oregano leaves, ground cumin seed, ground cinnamon, and ¼ teaspoon each ground cloves and pepper.

Cut 2½ to 3 pounds boneless lean top sirloin (trimmed of any fat) into 1½-inch cubes and place in the marinade, turning to coat all sides. Cover and refrigerate 2 to 4 hours.

You'll need to start the barbecue fire at least ½ to ¾ hour before you plan to serve in order to have an evenly ignited, solid bed of glowing coals. Lift meat cubes from marinade and thread equally on 4 to 5 metal skewers. If you need to expand servings, also thread additional skewers with sausages.

Arrange skewers on a barbecue grill about 4 inches above the glowing coals. Grill, turning often, until beef is browned on all sides and done to your liking (about 10 to 15 minutes for medium-rare). Cook sausages just until browned and hot through (about 10 minutes).

Transfer meats to a serving board and remove skewers. Slice sausages into thick pieces. Place several steak cubes (and some sausage slices, if used) in a warm flour tortilla (directions for heating follow). Top with heated canned refried beans and guacamole, if desired, and fold to enclose filling. Eat with your fingers. Makes 6 to 8 servings.

Warm Flour Tortillas

Stack 12 (1 package) flour tortillas and wrap tightly in foil. Place in a 350° oven for about 15 minutes (or place on the barbecue grill with meat for about 25 minutes, turning frequently) or until warm and soft.

Fourth-of-July Salmon

Barbecued Butterflied Salmon

Soy Butter Sauce

Corn on the Cob   Cherry Tomatoes

Buttered French Bread

Ice Cream Cones with Candy Toppings

You can present most of this meal for 10 to 12 from the barbecue: lightly smoked, slowly cooked salmon, the rich sauce, corn, and buttered French bread.

Start the barbecue early enough so the coals have about 30 minutes to ignite fully. Slice and butter 1 or 2 loaves of French bread and wrap in foil to heat with the fish for about the last 30 minutes. Remove the husks and silk from the corn, allowing 1 ear for each serving. If your barbecue is large enough, wrap the corn in foil to cook alongside the salmon for 1 hour or cook in boiling salted water in the kitchen.

Dessert, planned with children in mind, can be prepared ahead of time. Scoop ice cream balls and freeze on a flat pan until time to serve. Crush hard candies, such as peanut brittle or hard toffees (allow about 1 tablespoon for each serving). Present ice cream in an insulated container; have sugar cones alongside. Invite guests to assemble their own ice cream cones, spooning crushed candies over the ice cream.

Barbecued Butterflied Salmon

Have your fishman trim off head, tail, and back fin of a 6 to 8-pound salmon, butterfly the salmon from the stomach side, and bone it, leaving skin intact. Trim any white-colored membrane from the inside belly area of the fish. Lay the salmon out, skin side down, on heavyduty foil. Cut the foil to follow the outline of the fish.

Place salmon on foil on a grill 8 inches above a single layer of totally ignited, gray-colored coals (arrange coals to cover all the area below the fish). If necessary, add a few more previously ignited coals as fish cooks. Brush salmon with 3 tablespoons melted butter or margarine and cover lightly with a large sheet of foil forming a small dome. Start checking salmon after 45 minutes; then check about every 10 minutes. When done, salmon flakes readily with a fork in the thickest portion.

Supporting fish with foil, slip it onto a large serving board or platter. To serve, lift pieces of salmon from foil with a spatula (the skin adheres to the foil). Accompany with Soy Butter Sauce (recipe follows), but add sparingly because it is pungently flavored. Makes 10 to 12 servings.

Soy Butter Sauce

In a small saucepan, melt ¾ cup (⅜ lb.) butter or margarine. Stir in 2 cloves minced or mashed garlic, 1½ tablespoons each soy sauce and dry mustard, ⅓ cup Sherry or regular-strength chicken broth, and 3 tablespoons catsup. Keep warm on the barbecue with the salmon. Makes 1½ cups.

Armenian Picnic

Armenian Hamburgers

Yogurt Relish

Eggplant and Vegetable Kebabs

Rice Pilaf with Je-hezz

Fresh Vegetable Salad

Peda, Sweet French, or Arabic Bread

Spiced Butter

Serve big, juicy Armenian Hamburgers from the barbecue for this picnic. You can season the hamburgers, mix the Yogurt Relish, and make the fruit topping for the rice the day before.

About 2 hours before dinner, start the pilaf. Then, about an hour before dinner, you may want to enlist help of other picnickers in preparing the vegetable kebabs, making the salad, setting the table, and preparing the barbecue. Allow ½ hour for a good bed of coals to form. Heat fruit topping for the rice while the meat grills.

For Spiced Butter, add 1 teaspoon ground allspice to ½ pound soft butter or margarine; serve in a crock or small dish.

Armenian Hamburgers

Buy equal amounts of ground lamb and ground beef. To each pound of meat, add about 2 tablespoons each finely minced or ground celery, green pepper, and parsley; ½ cup ground or finely minced onion; and 1 teaspoon seasoned salt. Knead together until well blended, gradually adding about 3 tablespoons water. Shape each pound of meat into 3 or 4 patties.

Grill burgers about 6 inches above moderately-hot coals until they're well browned on both sides; it takes about 8 to 10 minutes total time for medium-rare. Then season them to taste with additional salt and pepper. Each pound of meat makes 3 or 4 servings.

(Continued on next page)

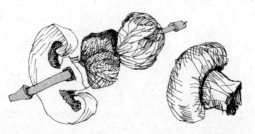

Yogurt Relish

Combine in a bowl 3 cups unflavored yogurt; 6 green onions (including some of the green tops), sliced thin; 1 large clove garlic, minced or mashed; and 2 teaspoons finely crushed dried mint (or 4 teaspoons finely chopped fresh mint). Stir until blended, cover, and refrigerate for at least 4 hours or overnight. Season lightly with salt before serving. Makes 12 servings.

Eggplant and Vegetable Kebabs

Rinse 2 medium-sized (about 1¼ lbs. each) eggplants, cut off stem ends, and cut into chunks about 2 inches square. Sprinkle lightly with salt and drain in a colander for about 30 minutes. Also rinse 4 large green peppers, slice off stem ends, remove seeds, and cut in 2-inch squares. And have ready 3 large onions, peeled and sliced lengthwise into thin strips, and 1 pound medium-sized mushrooms, wiped, trimmed and cut in quarters. You'll need about ⅔ cup olive oil or butter and salt and pepper.

On the barbecue or on your range, heat about ¼ cup oil or butter in a 12-inch frying pan. Add onions and sauté, stirring often, until limp. Then add mushrooms and sauté until most of the mushroom juices are absorbed. Meanwhile, arrange eggplant and green pepper pieces alternately on 3 to 4 long skewers. Brush generously with oil or melted butter and place over coals; keep turning until eggplant is soft and well charred (takes 25 to 30 minutes). Push off skewers into the sautéed onion mixture. Continue sautéing all the vegetables together for about 5 more minutes, adding salt and pepper to taste. Keep warm on side of grill for serving. Makes about 12 servings.

Rice Pilaf with Je-hezz

Ahead of time prepare fruit and nuts for Je-hezz topping: sauté ¼ pound whole blanched almonds in about 1 tablespoon butter over low heat, stirring until evenly golden brown; drain on paper towels. Rinse and pat dry ¼ pound raisins or currants. Snip ¼ pound each dried apricots and pitted dates in quarters; set aside.

Start pilaf about 1½ hours before serving time. In a 5-quart pan, heat 5 cups regular-strength chicken broth to boiling with ¼ pound butter and ½ teaspoon each salt and sugar. Add 2 cups long grain rice and cook, stirring, until mixture returns to boiling. Reduce heat, cover, and simmer for 15 minutes. Then turn rice mixture into a 2½-quart casserole, cover, and put into a 325° oven for 1 hour or until serving time. (Pack hot dish in an insulated bag or wrap well in newspapers for a picnic away from home.) Keep hot on side of grill.

Finish Je-hezz over grill. Heat 2 tablespoons butter in a 10-inch frying pan. Put in raisins and turn until heated through; then add dates and turn in butter. Add apricots and stir until fruits are heated through. Just before serving, pour fruits over pilaf, then sprinkle with toasted almonds. Makes 12 servings.

Fresh Vegetable Salad

Cut 4 medium-sized tomatoes into ½ to ¾-inch dice, discarding seed pockets. Dice 2 green peppers and 2 regular (or 1 Armenian) cucumber. Combine in a bowl with 2 cups sliced celery and ¾ cup chopped fresh parsley.

Also prepare mint dressing: combine 2 tablespoons crushed dried mint (or ¼ cup finely chopped fresh mint) with 2 teaspoons salt, ¼ teaspoon cayenne, and 1 teaspoon ground cumin. Add ⅓ cup olive oil and 1 to 2 tablespoons lemon juice, mix to blend.

Just before serving, add dressing to vegetables and mix lightly. Garnish with watercress or romaine or mix some of these greens into salad. Makes about 12 servings.

Pakistani-Style Barbecue

Spicy Barbecued Chicken

Tomato-Cucumber Sauce

Cracked Wheat Pilaf or
Chicken-flavored Rice Mix

Butter Lettuce Salad
Oil and Vinegar Dressing

Melon Wedges, Grapes, Figs

You slash each piece of chicken to allow the spicy hot marinade to penetrate deeply into the meat. Then the highly seasoned grilled chicken is served with a cooling sauce. If your tolerance for pepper is low, use the minimum amount of cayenne in the marinade.

Early in the day, or the night before, prepare the chicken and marinate it, covered, in the refrigerator; turn occasionally. The Tomato-Cucumber Sauce, salad greens, and fruit can also be fixed ahead and chilled.

Then while the chicken is cooking, make your favorite wheat or rice pilaf or prepare a rice mix according to package directions.

To serve, pass the Tomato-Cucumber Sauce to spoon over the chicken or offer each person a small bowl of the sauce to use for dipping each bite.

Spicy Barbecued Chicken

8 whole chicken legs, thighs and
   drumsticks attached
1 cup unflavored yogurt
1 teaspoon ground ginger
1 teaspoon garlic powder
½ to 1 teaspoon cayenne
1 teaspoon salt
¼ cup lemon juice
   Lemon wedges

Remove chicken skin, if you wish. Slash each piece of chicken 2 or 3 times about halfway to the bone; place in a shallow tight-fitting pan. Combine the yogurt, ginger, garlic powder, cayenne, salt, and lemon juice; pour over chicken, cover, and refrigerate 6 to 8 hours or overnight, turning occasionally.

Lift chicken from marinade, drain briefly, and place on a well-greased grill about 6 inches above a solid bed of low-glowing coals. Cook, turning and lightly brushing with marinade, until well browned on all sides and thigh meat is no longer pink next to the bone (about 40 to 50 minutes). Arrange on a serving platter and garnish with lemon wedges. Makes 8 servings.

Tomato-Cucumber Sauce

2 cups unflavored yogurt
2 medium-sized tomatoes, peeled and
   finely diced
1 medium-sized cucumber, peeled and
   finely diced
⅓ cup thinly sliced green onion,
   including the green tops
2 teaspoons ground cumin seed
1 teaspoon salt
2 tablespoons finely chopped fresh
   coriander (cilantro), watercress, or
   mint

Blend together the yogurt, tomatoes, cucumber, green onion, cumin, salt, and coriander. Cover and refrigerate for 2 to 4 hours or until thoroughly chilled. Makes about 4 cups, enough for 8 generous servings.

Barbecued Chicken and Shrimp Skewers

Chicken and Shrimp en Brochette
Fluffy White Rice
Whole Artichokes and Melted Butter
Quick Carob Cake

Here is an unusual way to feature the succulent dark meat of chicken legs and thighs. The chicken is combined with shrimp (sometimes sold as jumbo prawns) impaled on skewers. Serve them with fluffy rice and boiled, whole artichokes to dip in melted butter. The dessert is a quick-to-mix cake made with roasted carob powder (sold as a chocolate substitute in natural or health food stores). Make and bake it while the chicken and shrimp barbecue.

Chicken and Shrimp en Brochette

    4   each chicken legs and thighs (about
          2½ lbs.)
   12   large raw shrimp (about ¾ lb.)
   ¾   cup dry white wine
    2   tablespoons lemon juice
    3   tablespoons olive oil
    1   teaspoon Worcestershire
    2   large cloves garlic, minced or
          mashed
    1   teaspoon salt
   ⅛   teaspoon pepper
   ¼   teaspoon thyme leaves, crumbled
   ½   teaspoon rosemary leaves, crumbled
          Chopped parsley
   ¼   cup regular-strength chicken broth
    1   teaspoon cornstarch

Cut chicken legs and thighs apart, if necessary; place in a bowl. Peel and devein shrimp and add to chicken. Combine the wine, lemon juice, oil, Worcestershire, garlic, salt, pepper, thyme, and rosemary; pour over chicken and shrimp. Cover and refrigerate 2 to 4 hours, turning several times.

Lift chicken pieces from marinade; arrange on a barbecue grill about 6 inches above glowing coals. Grill until well browned on all sides and meat near bone is no longer pink (about 30 minutes). Turn and baste with marinade several times. Lift chicken from grill; cool slightly. When cool enough to handle, thread 1 leg and 1 thigh with 3 raw shrimp on each of 4 skewers.

Place skewers on grill and cook until shrimp are pink and tender, turning once and basting, a total of 8 to 10 minutes. Remove to a serving board; top with parsley and cover to keep warm.

Combine chicken broth and cornstarch; stir into remaining marinade and cook, stirring until bubbly and slightly thickened. Pass in a bowl to spoon over skewers. Serves 4.

Quick Carob Cake

   1½   cups all-purpose flour, unsifted
    1   cup sugar
   ¼   cup roasted carob powder
    1   teaspoon soda
   ½   teaspoon salt
   ⅓   cup salad oil
    1   tablespoon vinegar
    1   teaspoon vanilla
    1   cup cold water
          Fluffy Carob Frosting (directions
          follow)

Combine the flour, sugar, carob powder, soda, and salt; sift into a bowl. Make a well in the flour and pour in the salad oil, vinegar, vanilla, and cold water. Stir with a spoon just until blended.

Spread batter in a greased 9-inch-square baking pan. Bake in a 350° oven for about 25 minutes or until a pick inserted in the center comes out clean. Cool in the pan on a rack. Spread Fluffy Carob Frosting on top, if you wish. Makes about 8 servings.

Fluffy Carob Frosting. In the small bowl of your electric mixer, lightly beat 1 egg white. Add 3 tablespoons soft butter or margarine, a dash of salt, ¼ cup roasted carob powder, and ¼ teaspoon vanilla; beat until blended. Gradually add 1 cup sifted powdered sugar; beat until smooth and fluffy. Makes enough for an 8 or 9-inch-square cake.

Korean Short Ribs

Marinated Korean Short Ribs
Peas and Peanut Slaw
Sourdough French Bread
Butter

Korean cooks often select beef short ribs for barbecuing because they develop such a rich flavor. Cut crisscross through the short ribs for even cooking. It also helps insure juicy, tender meat.

Choosing meaty short ribs with the fat evenly distributed throughout the lean is important; those with obvious fat layers are less successful for barbecuing. You need to cook them over a low fire, and it may be necessary to devise a way to elevate your grill to the suggested 7 or 8 inches.

You can prepare the slaw and let it chill while the meat marinates or make it the night before. Slice and butter a long loaf of sourdough French bread to serve.

Marinated Korean Short Ribs

    4 pounds lean beef short ribs
    3 tablespoons soy sauce
    ½ cup dry red wine
    2 tablespoons firmly packed brown
       sugar
    3 green onions, chopped
    2 cloves garlic, minced or mashed
    3 slices fresh ginger root, each about
       ½ by 1 inch and ⅛ inch thick
    ¼ cup salad oil
    1 tablespoon toasted sesame seed

Have your meatman cut short ribs through bone into about 2½-inch lengths. At home, cut meat as follows: With bone side down, cut each rib through meat halfway to the bone at ½-inch intervals; repeat cuts at right angles to first cuts but make these cuts only ½ inch deep.

In a bowl mix the soy sauce, wine, brown sugar, green onions, garlic, ginger root, salad oil, and sesame seed. If desired, apply regular (not instant) tenderizer to ribs according to package directions; immediately put ribs into marinade, with cut side down, and let stand, covered, for about 2 hours (marinate only for 1 hour if using tenderizer).

Meanwhile, adjust barbecue so that meat will grill 7 to 8 inches above coals and prepare fire with about 30 briquets. When glowing coals form, spread them in an even layer large enough to accommodate ribs. Place ribs on grill, with bone side down. Turn ribs frequently and baste with marinade until well browned on all sides (about 30 minutes); the meat should be a faint pink inside (cut a gash next to bone to check). Makes 4 servings.

Peas and Peanut Slaw

Turn 1 package (10 oz.) frozen peas into a colander and run hot water over them to thaw; drain well. In a bowl combine the peas, 2 cups finely shredded cabbage, and 1 green onion (thinly sliced).

In a bowl blend ¼ cup each sour cream and mayonnaise with ¼ teaspoon each salt and curry powder, dash pepper, and 1 teaspoon each prepared mustard and wine vinegar. Pour over cabbage mixture and mix lightly. Cover and chill for at least an hour or overnight.

Before serving, pour ¾ cup salted, Spanish-style peanuts over top of salad. Makes 4 to 6 servings.

Pork on the Grill

Pork Tenderloin

Mellowed Turnips

Tossed Green Salad

Strawberry-Orange Refrigerator
Dessert

You'll need to start marinating the pork and make the dessert the day before.

"Mellowed Turnips" are a blending of rutabaga, carrots, yam, and jicama.

Pork Tenderloin

1½ to 2 pounds pork tenderloin
½ cup regular-strength chicken broth
½ cup soy sauce
¼ cup Japanese sake or dry Sherry
6 tablespoons sugar
1 clove garlic, minced or mashed
1 teaspoon red food coloring

Cut the pork across the grain into 2 or 3 equal pieces. Mix the broth, soy sauce, wine, sugar, garlic, and food coloring; pour over pork, cover, and marinate in the refrigerator for at least 24 hours, turning meat several times. Lift pork from marinade, drain briefly and arrange on the grill of a covered barbecue about 4 to 6 inches above a ring of low-glowing coals. Cover barbecue, adjust dampers, and cook about 25 minutes or until center of meat is no longer pink when slashed; turn and baste often. To serve, cut across the grain in thin slanting slices. Makes 4 to 6 servings.

Mellowed Turnips

1 large rutabaga (about ¾ lb.)
3 large carrots
1 large yam (about ¾ lb.)
  Water
⅔ cup peeled and finely diced jicama,
  or drained and diced water
  chestnuts
¼ cup (⅛ lb.) soft butter or margarine
½ teaspoon salt
¼ teaspoon pepper
⅛ teaspoon ground nutmeg
⅓ cup slivered almonds

Peel the rutabaga, carrots, and yam; cut into 1-inch chunks. Cover and cook the vegetables in a small amount of boiling water until very tender when pierced (about 25 minutes). Drain. Mash the vegetables with a potato masher or beat with an electric mixer until smooth; you should have 3 to 3½ cups. Stir in the jicama, butter, salt, pepper, and nutmeg until well blended; spoon into a 1 to 1½-quart shallow casserole. Sprinkle evenly with almonds. Bake, uncovered, in a 375° oven for 20 minutes or until heated through. Makes about 6 servings.

Strawberry-Orange Refrigerator Dessert

1 box (about 1 pint) strawberries
1 large orange
½ cup (¼ lb.) butter or margarine
1 cup unsifted powdered sugar
2 eggs
  About 28 vanilla wafers
3 tablespoons melted butter or
  margarine
1 cup (½ pt.) whipping cream

Rinse and dry berries. Cut the peel and all white membrane off orange; lift out sections and set aside.

Using an electric mixer, beat the ½ cup butter and sugar together until creamy. Add eggs, one at a time, and beat until fluffy.

Crush the vanilla wafers into fine crumbs (you should have 1 cup). Combine the crumbs and the melted butter; press into the bottom of a 9-inch-square baking dish. Spread the butter-egg mixture evenly over the crumb layer. Slice the berries (saving several whole berries for garnish) and mix gently with the orange sections; arrange over the butter mixture.

Whip the cream and spread over the fruit. Cover and refrigerate for at least 6 hours or overnight. Garnish with whole berries. Makes about 9 servings.

Week-End Barbecue

Grilled Steak

Corn on the Cob

Mustard Butter

Caesar Salad

French Bread

Chocolate-Coffee Freezer Torte

One thick steak that can be carved for 6 to 8 people is the center of this week-end barbecue dinner. A spicy Mustard Butter seasons both the meat and corn and also becomes a spread for the French bread, if you like.

You can make the torte days in advance and store it in the freezer. Then let it stand at room temperature about 15 minutes to soften slightly before serving. Also prepare the Mustard Butter ahead so it will have time to mellow. You'll need about 4 to 6 tablespoons of the butter to season the steak; pass the rest at the table for the corn and bread. And if you have any butter left, you can use it later as a sandwich spread.

Cook the corn as you wish—in the barbecue with the steak or in a large kettle of boiling water. Allow 1 or 2 ears of corn for each person, depending on appetites. Accompany the entrée with a Caesar salad.

Grilled Steak

Choose a large beef steak that will weigh 3 to 3½ pounds when cut about 2 inches thick. It could be porterhouse, top sirloin, or the first cut of top round (or buy a less tender cut such as sirloin tip or top round and use a commercial meat tenderizer as directed on the package).

Cook the steak on a grill about 6 inches above a bed of low-glowing coals. About every 10 minutes, turn it and spread the top lightly with about ½ tablespoon of the Mustard Butter (it will take about 40 minutes for rare steak). For best results, insert a meat thermometer in the center of the steak (after about 30 minutes) and cook until it registers 135° for rare or 140° for medium-rare to medium.

Remove to a serving platter and cut 5 or 6 crisscross slashes (about ¼ inch deep) in the top; spread with 1 to 2 tablespoons more Mustard Butter. To serve, cut across the grain in thin slanting slices. Makes 6 to 8 servings.

Mustard Butter

1 cup (½ lb.) soft butter or margarine
4 teaspoons dry mustard
1 teaspoon Worcestershire
¼ to ½ teaspoon garlic salt
⅛ teaspoon pepper
⅓ cup finely chopped parsley

In a bowl combine the butter, mustard, Worcestershire, garlic salt, pepper, and parsley; beat until smooth and well blended. Cover and refrigerate until needed. Makes about 1 cup.

(Continued on next page)

Chocolate-Coffee Freezer Torte

1 cup crushed coconut macaroon
    cooky crumbs
2 tablespoons melted butter or margarine
1 pint chocolate ice cream, slightly softened
½ cup chocolate-flavored syrup
1 pint coffee ice cream, slightly softened
    About 4 ounces chocolate-covered
    hard toffee candy bars, coarsely
    crushed

Stir together the cooky crumbs and butter. Lightly press into the bottom of a 9-inch cake pan with a removable bottom. Bake in a 350° oven for 8 to 10 minutes or until lightly browned. Cool.

Spread the chocolate ice cream in an even layer over the cooled crust; drizzle evenly with ¼ cup of the syrup and freeze until firm. Then top with an even layer of the coffee ice cream, sprinkle evenly with the crushed candy and drizzle remaining syrup over top. Cover and freeze until firm. Makes 6 to 8 servings.

Individual Stew on the Barbecue

Fruit Punch

Stew on the Barbecue

Warm Crusty Rolls

Shortbread Sundaes

This is a party planned for 6 to 8 guests. All the ingredients for the savory stew are either pre-cooked or quick-cooking so the entrée is ready to eat when hot and bubbly. They cook in individual foil dishes right on the grill. The meatballs for the stew can be prepared a day ahead (or freeze them for longer storage; then thaw before serving). You can also cook the potatoes ahead and assemble most of the vegetables several hours or a day ahead.

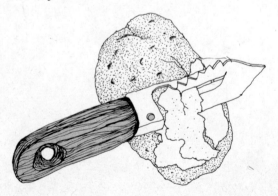

You'll also need to bake the shortbread cooky base for the dessert ahead. Guests assemble their own sundaes with the shortbread, ice cream, blueberries, cream, and nuts.

Wrap rolls in foil and set them to one side of the grill to warm while guests assemble their stew.

Individual Stew on the Barbecue

For the meatballs, combine 2 pounds lean ground beef, 2 eggs, ½ cup fine dry bread crumbs, 1 teaspoon dry mustard, and 2 teaspoons Worcestershire. Shape into balls the size of large marbles and arrange on rimmed baking pans. Bake in a 500° oven for 4 to 5 minutes or until browned. Refrigerate or freeze, if made ahead.

You'll also need about 1 to 1½ pounds fully cooked cocktail-sized frankfurters or smoke-flavored links.

Several hours or up to a day ahead, cook 1½ pounds unpeeled small red new potatoes in boiling water until tender; drain and chill. Then cut into chunks. Also thinly slice ¾ pound small white boiling onions (pick out fairly large-sized onions), separate into rings. Cut about ¾ pound carrots into paper-thin slices or coarsely shred; cover and chill.

Shortly before serving, thaw 1 package (10 oz. size) whole kernel corn or peas. And thinly slice ½-pound small fresh mushrooms.

For the Sauce, bring to simmering 2 large cans (15 oz. each) tomato sauce, 2 cans (about 14 oz. each) regular-strength beef broth, and 1 teaspoon each sugar, oregano and basil leaves; pour into a serving pitcher.

Place the meatballs, sausages, and vegetables in separate containers and arrange them near the barbecue with the pitcher of sauce. Also set out hot pads, a roll of foil, serving utensils, and a bowl of sour cream or grated Parmesan cheese.

Provide each guest with a small foil loaf pan (about 3¾ by 6 inches). Suggest they fill the pan about half-full with stew ingredients; then pour in enough sauce to almost cover stew. Cover pans with foil and set on grill about 4 to 6 inches above a medium-hot fire. The stew is ready to eat when bubbly hot (about 25 minutes). Remove from grill and stir in sour cream or grated Parmesan cheese, as desired. Serves 6 to 8.

Shortbread Sundaes

For the shortbread cooky base, combine 2¼ cups unsifted regular all-purpose flour, ½ cup sugar, and 1 cup (½ lb.) butter or margarine (cut in chunks). With your hands, work mixture until it

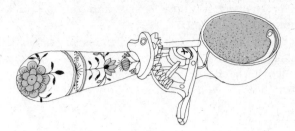

is very crumbly and no large particles remain; then press mixture into a firm lump with your hands. Place dough (it is crumbly) in a 9 by 13-inch baking pan and press out firmly and evenly. Impress edge of dough with tines of a fork; then carefully prick surface evenly. Bake in a 325° oven for about 30 minutes or until a pale golden brown. Remove from oven and, while hot, cut with a sharp knife into 6 to 8 pieces. Let cool in pan; then remove carefully with a wide spatula. (If made ahead, wrap airtight and store at room temperature.)

You'll also need about ½ gallon strawberry ice cream, about 2 cups blueberries, sweetened whipped cream, and toasted nuts. Serve buffet-style on dessert plates. Top shortbread with ice cream, blueberries, whipped cream, and toasted nuts, as desired.

Flank Steak Teriyaki

Barbecued Flank Steak

Fresh Green Vegetable

Combination White and Wild Rice

Ice Cream

Typical Japanese teriyaki seasonings flavor this juicy flank steak. Accompany with a fresh green vegetable of your choice and a packaged white and wild rice mix.

Barbecued Flank Steak

½ cup soy sauce
1 large clove garlic, minced or mashed
1 teaspoon ground ginger
2 tablespoons firmly packed brown sugar
2 tablespoons each lemon juice and salad oil
1 tablespoon instant minced onion
¼ teaspoon pepper
1 flank steak (about 1½ lbs.)

Combine the soy, garlic, ginger, brown sugar, lemon juice, salad oil, minced onion, and pepper. Place the steak in a close-fitting baking dish. Pour over the soy mixture, cover, and refrigerate 6 hours or overnight.

Turn the steak over several times so marinade can penetrate evenly.

To barbecue, place the steak on a grill about 4 inches above a bed of hot, glowing coals. Cook until nicely browned (about 6 minutes). Turn, baste with the marinade, and cook until browned and done to your liking (about 6 minutes longer for medium-rare).

To serve, cut thin, slanting slices diagonally across the grain of the steak. Serves 3 to 4.

Chicken on the Barbecue

Tossed Green Salad
Brussels Sprouts with Jack Cheese
Barbecued Breast of Chicken
Cherry Tomatoes   Celery Sticks
Ice Cream

This special method of cooking results in tender meat that's juicy and delicious. Success depends on cooking breasts quickly over hot coals; timing is very important.

Have the salad ready to serve when the chicken comes off the coals. For the vegetable dish, shred jack cheese over the hot, cooked sprouts for a quick sauce.

Serve crunchy celery sticks and firm cherry to-matoes for relishes. Scoops of your favorite ice cream finish off the meal.

Barbecued Breast of Chicken

8 very large chicken breasts (about ½ lb. each), split
About ¾ cup melted butter
About 1½ cups all-purpose flour
Salt and pepper
About ¼ cup melted butter or margarine

Rinse and dry chicken breasts thoroughly. Dip pieces, one at a time, into the ¾ cup melted butter; then shake in a paper bag with flour, seasoned with salt and pepper, to coat thoroughly. Place pieces on a greased grill 6 to 12 inches above hot coals or until opaque throughout (cut a gash to check). Cook 10 to 12 minutes on each side. Baste during cooking with about ¼ cup melted butter. Serve immediately. Makes 8 servings.

Index